GW01090302

LONDON'S 2ND CITY

CREATING CANARY WHARF

KEVIN D'ARCY

RAJAH BOOKS

First published
in the United Kingdom
in 2012 by Rajah Books
40 Bruce Road
London E3 3HL
020 8981 4691
rajahbooks@btopenworld.com

ISBN: 978-0-9556706-2-6

BIC categories:
855JPHV political structures, democracy
888JPR regional government

Printed and bound in Great Britain by
The MPG Group, Bodmin and King's Lynn.

The people who did it

Godfrey Hodgson
Paul Barker
Michael Heseltine
Geoffrey Howe
Peter Levene
Jack Dash
Michael von Clemm
G W Travelstead
Eduado Canet
Nigel Broakes
Reg Ward
Paul and Albert Reichmann
Eric Flounders/Brian Williams
George Iacobescu

INSIDE

THE PEOPLE

THE PLACE

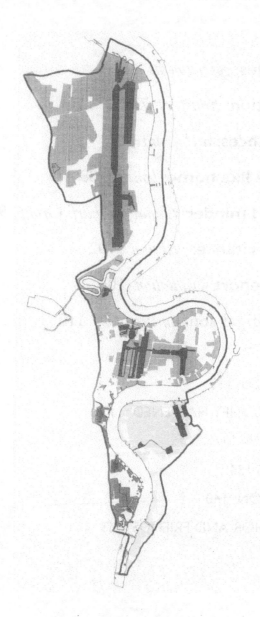

THE PLACE
Where a desert bloomed

FAMILY PLANNING
Themes

Either with or without a wedding, giving birth is a sensitive thing. In an ideal world this ought to happen only after considerable thought. In this case that had certainly happened, but not all the parties had the same idea of the most desirable outcome. And that was because, very roughly speaking, you could say there were four main parties involved and the communication between them all was, to put it mildly, casual.

The principal party was national government. After that, in any order, you have local government, the people, and business. The chapters that follow are designed to help the reader decide which party won and whether, when this happens again, it could be handled rather better.

Anyway, suddenly it happened. For many years after the second world war few people had heard of the Isle of Dogs. Even fewer people knew where it was. If you searched on the map it looked quite bare. Then, within twenty years, it had reappeared, as a brand new and gleaming city, expanded beyond the Isle of Dogs along the river to east and west. Nothing quite like it has happened before in any European country. Nothing so big, so fast, so dramatic.

Eight square miles of neglected land, divided by generous stretches of water, a strong stone's throw from the City of London, had been reborn as a City Mark Two to everyone's amazement. It was twice as big as the cities of London and Westminster put together.

Despite many dozens of publications, mainly explaining the cost to politicians (said to have been £8bn, but more likely to have been at least three times that) those like me who live in the East End, who are now quite impressed by our new relation, are still slightly dazed by what has happened and are not at all sure who did it. Or why. Or how. Or when. Hence this personal exploration.

My mother's father was a Barnardo boy, an orphan cockney from the East End of London. He never learned to read, but could count. That helped him make a lot of money, selling food off barrows, then through wholesale and imports, then setting up house in posh west London and profiting from property.

He never forgot his roots, though. Long after his death I moved to the East End and discovered what he had left behind. The aftermath of the second world war, when so many bombs had fallen on the docklands, had left the occasional pie and mash shop, but very little else. Much desolation and a lot of decay, scattered between some ancient examples of buildings at their best. But the cockney spirit, in many ways, was obvious enough to remind me of someone who had climbed his way to the top of the business he had nurtured all his life.

And what would my grandfather think of all this? I can see him drawing on a fat cigar, very slowly, without a word. He would pretend he was not jealous.

THE CRADLE
The East End

Where a child is born is always important. Canary Wharf is part of a borough more obviously vibrant than much of London. The borough of Tower Hamlets. Think more art galleries than anywhere else. Think the most improved schools in the country. Think of Brick Lane, Spittlefields and Houndsditch. Some aim to call Houndsditch 'Silicone Roundabout', in recognition of the concentration of high tech and creative industries. Others refer to the Houndsditch effect, the humanisation of buildings.

Think scores of wine bars, nightclubs and restaurants. Think the stately Tower of London. Think the country's best teaching hospitals with a history of Nobel prize winners. Think the lowest crime rate in the capital. Think public transport around the clock and speedy access to central London. Think competitive stores and shops and many more lively street markets than most. Think canals and miles of parks. And the new child, the city, Canary Wharf.

But why a city? In Britain a city is normally a town with an Anglican cathedral, to which the sovereign, head of both church and state, has been pleased to issue a royal charter. This, then, makes it a city. A bit of religious one-upmanship. But in recent years the tradition has been broken. Cathedrals are now no longer essential. .

But apart from that, what else is a city? A bigger than conventional town? A network binding everyone together? Yes, but also a vibrant place where people are inspired by being so close. A concentrated social organism. The bigger the area the bigger the concentration. All cities produce more energy and wealth at a markedly lower cost. A recent assessment says city people are 15 percent more productive than anyone else. This is partly because the cost of delivering services is obviously lower in a built-up area, sometimes by up to 50 percent. But the population is often younger and comparatively better educated. This is boosted by immigration, repeated over many years, constantly sparking existing residents to rethink basic assumptions. Most people who live in London were born in other places.

The great, sprawling region of greater London now covers a large chunk of south east England, with a population of 7.8m (1.6m working in financial services) and has an influence far beyond, both socially and politically.

The English elsewhere, and the Scots and Welsh, have long complained about London, The Great Wen, commanding an unfair share of influence, although they seldom complain of its income being generously spread elsewhere. Much of Britain is a drain on the state. London is a gross contributor. This is called a fiscal surplus and at the last count meant that £25.9bn was given to the rest of the country.

Victorian slums are ancient history. Those were the days of the famous London fog, fuelled by millions of coal-fired chimneys. Also the days of the London cough, creating the nasal intonation essential to the London accent. And also the days of blackened buildings, which have now been replaced by scrubbed white stone.

Living standards have improved immensely, meaning income, health and education, plus holidays abroad. Overcrowding is still recorded, but much of this seems to be local cheating to boost the electoral rolls. East London now is a different place from that recorded by Charles Dickens. The villains' dens were replaced by greenery and rows of modern housing. For instance, East End's Victoria Park. But for some its geography is still not clear. If you took, say, BBC news as a reference you might well think that deepest Essex is also an essential part of the East End. We in Tower Hamlets are not confused: the East End is definitely us.

All the same it would be too naïve to pretend that any part of London could exist without the rest. Many parts have clear identities created by numerous nationalities. The Irish in Hammersmith, the Indians in Newham, the French in Kensington, and so on. When I first moved to the East End, to Stepney, my neighbours were mainly Russian Jews of the second or third generation. Lenin had been a local tenant.

The very first banks, the grandest churches were largely the work of Flemish merchants. All of this provided evidence for the International Olympic Authority describing London as the world's leading multicultural city. The mayor of the Greater London Authority, personally boasting Turkish origins, certainly did not protest.

Gallup, in a poll of 38 cities, recently reported that London is seen by innovative people as their most attractive city. At 13 percent it came ahead of Paris at 8.5 percent, Barcelona at 6 percent, Berlin at 5 percent, and Rome and Stockholm, both at 3 percent. An impressive 40 percent of employed immigrants to Britain are classified as highly skilled, which seems an international record, and clearly most head for London. It is the most popular city in Europe for tourists.

In another poll the accountants PriceWaterhouseCoopers found that London ranked fourth for intellectual capital, behind New York, Paris and Tokyo, and third for ease of doing business after Singapore and Hong Kong, but first in the world for economic clout, however that is measured.

To Londoners' surprise, PWC also reports that London is ranked as the world's best city for transport and infrastructure, largely because of continual regeneration, as seen in Canary Wharf.

Many do not seem to have noticed the growth of the train map in recent years, primarily to the east of London. This explosion of public transport is not the result of idle doodling by civil servants in remote Whitehall, but is the product of an evolving economy, promoted by central direction. Michael Heseltine fought hard in cabinet for the Crossrail link to be routed through docklands and not, as British Rail had planned, to steer it through the south of London. And now all that is happening.

THE HOME
Reaction

I t would be wrong to think that London's second City sprang from totally virgin soil, even after the wartime bombing. Of course there was little trace of the business that was once the biggest docks in the world, with all the activity that goes alongside.

There were few decent structures, but still strong signs of an established culture, with roots going back many hundreds of years. These did not grow from, nor need, any buildings. The culture was very much deeper than that and its creation had a logic.

The business of moving goods in and out had grown in type and size and complexity. In the nineteenth century trade through London was greater than all of France, Germany and Italy together and four times that of the United States. Gradually London docks, once open to all, were overtaken by docks that were closed, in an effort to stem the amount of theft attracted by so much temptation. Security meant imposing walls, firmly linked by giant gates, and the subsequent isolation of docks from even those next door.

The use of labour was largely casual, with workers enlisted on a daily basis, selected from queues in the early morning outside public houses at the gates of the docks. The exploitation that this created led naturally to workers' unions which were grouped mainly by particular skills but which, all the same, encouraged an attitude of Them, the employers, and the workers, Us.

Physically, also, the Isle of Dogs was connected to the rest of London by just two roads, each with a swing bridge to open for shipping, the equivalent of gates. The trains were just for commercial use. There were only two occasional buses. Trams and trolley buses passed nearby, but not to the Isle of Dogs. Physical contact with the wider world was subsequently slight. There was no cinema and very few pubs, fewer shops, few doctors or schools.

It is hardly surprising that the rest of London had little awareness of life in the docks and that many of those who lived in the area were just as ignorant of the rest of London, as well as of the dock next door. So, separation by area and skills. Insularity became the norm, balanced by an equal need to gather your friends around you. While the closed nature of the docking business, with many jobs passing from father to son, suggesting therefore a job for life, inspired little urge for education, so little awareness of a richer existence or other ways of life. The belief that the docks gave a real education, as good as any university, had already lasted for generations. It was part of the cockney soul.

This was natural recruiting land for the newly emergent Labour Party and its sympathy for the working man. In 1892 the party had seen the election of its first member of Parliament, Keir Hardie, for East Ham, which was spiritually if not actually in the East End. East Ham also later boasted Britain's first council in Labour control. Also the national voice of the party, the *Daily Herald*, owed much to the mayor of (then) the London Borough of Poplar, George Lansbury. He later led the Labour Party. This all helped nurture an east London ethos, a kind of conservative socialism. But it also ensured that its members in the area would find it hard to support the party as it later became more middle class. Reaction to any form of change, especially if not explicitly for the working class, strengthened by the day. This hardened with increasing encouragement by Communists during dock disputes, which meant that Labour-led trade unions were equally dismayed, while unemployed workers could employ their free time planning ever more devious defiance. The epithet that stung most fiercely was the description of the area by a Conservative politician as 'a hotbed of Labour Loonies'.

(A Teniell cartoon in the early *Punch* magazine showed two cockneys, one saying to the other 'Ere comes a stranger, eave alf a brick at im'. Malcolm Muggeridge, editor in the 1950s, said that this typified a national habit he was determined to resist.)

The reactionary attitude was understandably nursed by members of the local councils, elected of course by the local majority. This encouraged others to dig in their heels. The docklands plainly needed improvement. This was clear to those who did not live there. Those who did live there needed help to prevent and overcome decay. But there was also economic reaction. Those controlling most of the land - docks, gasworks, railways and so on - were reluctant to agree in any way on how to improve the area physically. They preferred to sit on their hands and wait to be paid large sums to go away, encouraged by seeing property prices rise by the day.

The more politicians tried to move on by better utilisation of land, the more local resistance grew. This was partly for instinctive reasons, but also for strategic reasons: here was a movement worth resisting for the sake of winning particular battles, if only for the bribes. When change did happen, in later years, resisters formed interest groups, shadowing normal political movements, sometimes working in coalition, sometimes very much not.

This was confused in the 1970s by a sudden surge of Bangladeshi families arriving to join their husbands or sons. They came from a poorly educated country with little grasp of legality or democracy and, at first, little grasp of English. Politics, for them, was mainly a matter of supporting neighbours you know, plus friends. Being elected was a form of reward, not anything needing action. It would take some time to change this. Dacca-on-Thames has for many years been central to the East End.

Some lucky people would be more comfortable. Those like photographer Lord Snowden, husband to Princess Margaret; Sir David Lean, the film director; Lord David Owen, co-founder of the short-lived Social Democratic and Liberal Party with other members of the Limehouse Four; and Daniel Farson, the Anglo-American who was a feted homosexual and anti-establishment journalist and host at

The Waterman's Arms. They all lived for a while in picturesque property with pleasant views of the Thames. The notorious criminals and sadists, the Kray brothers, were close: I published an interview with them in *London Life*, the bible of swinging London.

This was the culture that still existed when the future finally did arrive, in what was a physical and mental desert, instinctively fearful of the wider world and its power of exploitation.

It was not the happy home best suited for the birth of a healthy child.

THE BIRTH

Process

No birth is painless. Some can be awful. The birth of Canary Wharf took place in fits and starts over several years with no abortion or caesarean section - but only just.

You may well believe that, in the region called London, administered by the Greater London Authority, that the most important city after the City of London has to be, to the west, Westminster. Technically, indubitably, yes. It is legally a city and it certainly houses some major institutions, such as Whitehall, Parliament and Buckingham Palace. But for me the beating heart of a capital is where the major business is done. And this, for me, is the city I am calling Canary Wharf, reborn to the east in 1981, covering more land than both the City and Westminster and home to the bulk of the financial services that firmly motor Britain.

I have always been bemused by the fact that many Britons, rightly proud of the industrial revolution, are reluctant to accept that service industries have always earned more than manufacturing. London leads the world in financial centres, ahead of New York, Hong Kong and Singapore. Frankfurt comes in sixth.

Three quarters of our income comes from services in general, while exports of financial services saw a fivefold increase between 1992 to 2009, to a record £24.4bn. In the past ten years Britain has attracted more emerging market investment, after the US, than any other country. For instance, most of the world's biggest mining companies have moved their headquarters to London.

Two fifths of the world's foreign exchange moves through London. Hedge fund activity is second only to the US. And London leads the world in cross-border bank lending, as well as marine insurance.

In terms of financial sector workers (lawyers and accountants, as well as bankers) it is true that the City of London can claim three times more than Canary Wharf's 100,000, but the first has little room to expand, while the second has a lot. Westminster, at the last count, had a modest 60,000 workers.

I use Canary Wharf as a label, not so much as a real address. At the centre it has the Isle of Dogs, what some still call the Island. And before that Stebun (or Stepney) Marsh, drained of water by seven windmills (in Millwall) in the 1600s. Now I see it as The City Mark Two. Some have called it Wall Street on Thames, more for architectural reasons than for its North American tenants. But what has happened here over twenty years has also affected a wider area, on both sides of the river. It especially affected the City of London, founded way back in 50 AD, but has also reached many miles beyond, into what some now bravely call the Thames Gateway.

Economists for the Halifax Bank says that central east London, by which they mean Tower Hamlets, Hackney and

Southwark, showed a higher increase in economic activity from 1998 to 2008 than anywhere else in Britain. This is because of a rise in average personal income by 87 percent from £17,902 to £33,499. True, the City Mark One has a higher average income, but shows a very much lower increase. And as the Halifax survey started from the year when the London Docklands Development Corporation officially came to the end of its life the cause and effect are clearly linked. The catalyst was Canary Wharf.

I have lived and worked here throughout this newest birth and development. It is interesting to see today how those now briefed to tell the story appear to believe that this motley mass of gargantuan, glazed, somewhat Disney-like structures could have been the product of a virgin birth that happened overnight.

The result, all the same, was miraculous. An awkward child, but a healthy one. It is the product of determined effort by a wide collection of eager sponsors who finally shared a common aim. And this despite a wealth of opposition from many neighbours on many levels, from many walks of life. It is also despite an impressive number of predictable mistakes. City Mark Two is a comparatively young 30 year old. There are clearly lessons here to be learned. New cities will always grow.

In the beginning Canary Wharf was a virtual desert. What had become the London Docks and the hungry mouth of the British Empire, consuming goods from all over the world, was a major target in the second world war for invading enemy aircraft. Endless streams of bombs were dropped. Few houses were untouched. The aim was to bring British trade to a stop in what had been the world's biggest port, with over 100,000 workers, one fifth of London's manpower. The result was a massive loss of life, with more than 2,000 killed or injured and the loss of 10,000 modest houses, many of which housed three families. After the war the docks wound down. The shift from boxes to container transport called for ships very much too large for a port designed by the ancient Romans. And so for years it stood neglected.

City Mark One was a lot less damaged. That special centre of superiority, which had grown over years on the back of trade, picked itself up and quickly remembered its dreams of future grandeur. It had never had much time for democracy and it is still part driven by its old trade guilds, conditioned to funding bankrupt kings in return for independence. The sovereign must still ask permission to visit. Ancient attitudes die hard. Its revival was helped by the state relaxing the laws on financial services in such a way as to make The Square Mile attractive to money men worldwide and especially those in the USA, where trading rules were stricter. So it grew, and grew, and grew.

Like a giant in a fairy story, though, it grew so much that it almost burst. A square mile was simply not enough. Demand for office space had created the most expensive property in the world. And there was not enough space for the open plan offices increasingly needed for the business of finance. Meanwhile, the Isle of Dogs was sleeping, windy, wet and undisturbed. Local musicians, Mike and Kate Westbrook, walked for hours in the tracks of old streets and composed a jazz song of forgotten London, evidence of a long gone empire with strange, exotic, foreign names: the Indies, Malacca and so on. Decaying warehouses still released fumes of ginger and walnut, allspice and rum.

Some thirty years of decline in the docklands was accelerated through industrial action by what remained of shipping activity. Strikes were followed by further strikes. My neighbour, Jack Dash, the dockers' leader, later said that he had been misused by political activists determined to kill any sensible deal. By then he had stopped fighting social improvement and protesting at the greening of the area and started to study fine art. But decline had become an addiction.

THE PARENTS

Origination

t is easy to believe that that Canary Wharf was all the product of just one body, the London Docklands Development Corporation - the LDDC. Or the product of just one man, Reg Ward, the first chief executive. Or of one politician, Michael Heseltine. Or of one developer, Paul Reichmann. But who remembers Gooch Ware Travelstead, Michael von Clemm, Godfrey Hodgson, Paul Barker? And what of Lord Levene?

I've spent much time plunging into the mountains of evidence, a lot of which is self-contradictory, so that this account should at least be different and, hopefully, more accurate.

Norman McCrae, deputy editor of *The Economist* for years, used to say that statistics and politics are totally pointless when they are separated from real life. Charles Dickens, as the editor of *Household Words*, made a similar comment in 1854: 'Political economy is a mere skeleton unless it has a little human covering'. What follows are my examples of suitable clothing.

What is certainly true is that organisations are only as good as the people in them. It can be nice for those within groups to pretend either that they don't do anything or that everything happens because of them, depending on the audience. The truth is always a mixture, of course. So naming the father of London's second City can never be an easy task. I would say that there was more than one.

Forging a future for the Isle of Dogs had been tried well before the LDDC. There were many earnest folks involved, such as local politicians. The largest group involved at the time were working in the Greater London Council, which took over from the London County Council in 1965. In the same year a new borough was created out of Poplar, Stepney and Bethnal Green and given the title of Tower Hamlets. (The tower bit came from the Tower of London, the hamlets came from ancient history. No matter, it was still the East End.)

The Isle of Dogs included docks run by the Port of London Authority, which also ran docks elsewhere in the Thames in the boroughs of Newham and Southwark. This whole wider area was, of course, most generally called the Docklands.

As world freight was being moved from cargo boats to container goliaths, the PLA saw that its future business was not going to be in the narrow Docklands, so they wanted to move down river. The GLC bought St Katherine's Dock, bang next to Tower Bridge, to develop hotels and a glitzy yacht harbour. Surrey Docks were sold to Southwark Council, which began to fill them in. And so on.

Already you can see that the power to decide on what to do was not up to one group. Most land was owned by the public, through local councils, the PLA, British Rail, British Gas, and so on. The trouble with that was that few of these bodies needed to bother with the opinion of the public. The councils, of course, were elected by the people, but the others were run like private companies with policies of their own. These all wanted to leave the area, but they also wanted to see, by waiting, if the value of their land would rise, so producing a bigger income.

There was no problem in drawing up plans on what to do with the land, once vacant. The problem was making it happen. Indeed, there were so many plans produced, and so many efforts to consult the public, at least by elected politicians, that people began to complain. (Oh no, not another survey!)

The problem was mainly twofold. One was the lack of any body with power enough to force through action, regardless of what other bodies thought. The other was the traditional problem of who was going to pay. There was nothing about the Isle of Dogs that said it was an obvious place for profitable investment. Residents were leaving, jobs were going, and the amount of decay was getting so bad that the likely cost of sorting it out was frightening to consider. There was little transport, few facilities, and hardly anyone buying anything, and it was worsening by the day. The general feeling was that anywhere else would be bound to produce a better return, for either public or private money. The odds were that a second city would never be conceived.

Luckily there is no monopoly in the sketching out of good ideas. Some thoughtful journalists and their knowledgeable friends were having some thoughts of their own. In 1961 an article was published in a Conservative magazine called *Crossbow* by one Godfrey Hodgson. (He later became famous at *The Sunday Times* and, later, on Channel Four, not to mention Oxford and Harvard. He also became more left wing.) He had become distressed by the growing number of valuable but declining towns and argued the case for moving the initiative for dealing with this from local authorities, who usually lacked resources. He launched the idea of national agencies to deal with urban regeneration as an arm of national government. The national government was then Conservative, but they failed to take it on board.

Later, in 1969, a left-wing weekly, *New Society*, carried a similar piece by the editor, Paul Barker, working with town planners and architects, effectively saying that the best development could only happen with a lot less planning. They even called it the Non-Plan. Unfortunately this did not stop the Greater London Development Plan being produced that year by the Labour-led GLC, helped by a Labour national government. Nor did it stop a plan for the Docklands produced by the civil engineers Travers Morgan in 1973. Nor a 20-year strategic plan for the Docklands in 1976. The Labour government was also advised to set up a development corporation for the Docklands, but they chose to let that slide, thank goodness.

Happily there are some politicians who keep a file of bright ideas and bring them out when needed. One such was the Conservative Geoffrey Howe who launched a plan both in and for the Docklands in 1978, derived, he admitted, from

Hodgson's article, for what he then called Enterprise Zones. These would be small but crucial areas quite free of red tape and normal taxation for a limited number of years. The flying start that this would give to companies should get the ball rolling for others, he thought. The idea is now used in many countries, from the US to Singapore.

The next year, 1979, saw the Conservatives win a national election, when at least one seed for London's second city was well and truly planted. An all-party committee of politicians grilled the Docklands Joint Committee (that's the GLC and five London boroughs) and pointed out that they had wasted five years by achieving exactly nothing.

Then Geoffrey Howe became the Chancellor. Immediately his colleague, Michael Heseltine, announced urban development corporations, to work alongside Enterprise Zones, but mainly distinguished by being all-powerful and not demanding plans. Paul Barker should take a modest bow. And also Godfrey Hodgson.

Passing the legislation through Parliament brought opposition from London politicians, dominated by the Labour Party (after all, the corporation was to steal their land), but eventually members of The House of Lords granted the process their approval. Something new had to be tried, they said.

Finally, in 1981, the LDDC was up and running. In fact, core staff were employed before that, a good eighteen months, to save on time. An empty warehouse was furnished with crates that played the part of desks.

Plainly, London's second city can claim a number of different parents, all sowing seeds at different times, but there was little doubt that a lively infant was close to being born.

Michael Heseltine

THE GODFATHER
Development

The godfather lived for seventeen years. There was life before and now there's life after. But there is little doubt that City Mark Two could never have happened otherwise. It was the principal motor for change. The London Docklands Development Corporation was politically created by Michael Heseltine, blessed by prime minister Margaret Thatcher. With a certain amount of original thought, as we've seen, from various outsiders, plus a series of various ministers, such as John Wakeham, Paul Channon and Cecil Parkinson. It started in 1981.

Throughout its life the Corporation faced opposition for political reasons. As a bullish initiative by a Conservative national government, impatient at decades of local inaction, the local London Labour governments tried every device to confuse and defeat it. This included the four local councils directly affected by the Corporation, as well as the Greater London Council before Mrs Thatcher killed it in 1986.

It was not that the councils were opposed to development. It was rather the way that they had hoped to see it, and had tried for some years to make it happen, was driven mainly by preoccupation with their existing familial responsibilities, with the biggest aim, as they saw it, to improve provision of what was then called council housing.

The East End of London, as with many cities, attracted

many low income earners, including a heavy flow of immigrants. Overcrowding was a serious problem, dragging down health and education, and there was more than the normal proportion of homeless, not to mention the unemployed. You could understand how socialists, with their prime concern the underprivileged, would centre on this social policy. There was also the matter of votes.

But the Conservative government, with its grander incentive of trying to boost the national income, saw this desert to the east of the capital as a bigger opportunity.

I once worked for Michael Heseltine, when he bought a magazine I worked on, then called *Man about Town*. It eventually ended up called *Town* and was aimed at creating a brand new market for young men with easy money to spend. Like Heseltine. A little bit ahead of its time, the brilliant star inevitably faded, but not before I saw his ability to play his cards very close to his chest, while determined still to win.

More recently I talked to Heseltine about his work on Canary Wharf and he reminded me that it all came about almost, you could say, by accident. As a government minister he had become concerned with the neglected space on the south bank of the Thames, either side of the Festival Hall, then a concrete memorial to the Festival of Britain so many years before. He used a helicopter to get a better view and in the course of that became aware of the area, even bigger, even more neglected, to the east of Tower Bridge.

Back at the office he asked his officials to create a system to end the stalemate brought about by the reluctance to work together by the many public bodies in the area, by taking a national initiative. He was told that national government could, but not if the process was created for a single borough. The initiative had to be taken in the national interest. Right, he said, so let's include Liverpool. And that was how it began.

Toxteth in Liverpool may be grateful, but the result there since then cannot compare with the result in Canary Wharf. And the reason for that could well be the success (you could call it luck) of Canary Wharf in attracting emerging wealth.

Oddly, however, this came about once again almost accidentally, possibly by an individual doing a Heseltine and seizing an opportunity. Three years after the corporation was born the LDDC chief executive was doing his best to wine and dine important people on a floating restaurant in one of the docks and – suddenly – it worked. His guest that day was a US banker, Michael von Clemm, the chairman of Credit Suisse First Boston, who also chaired Roux Brothers, a London restaurant contemplating mass production and needing premises for expansion. Also present was Archibald Cox, chairman of the bankers Morgan Stanley. Reg Ward, chief executive of LDDC, pointed to the available space in Shed 31 on the dockside. Ideal for preparing food, he said. And it was next to the shed producing television like Spitting Image, famous in its time for political satire.

Michael von Clemm was the man who, at Merrill Lynch, had invented the Eurobond market, together with Stanislas Yassukovich of White, Weld and Company. The supremely elegant Yassukovich was a Polish American who combined investment banking with being Master of the Quorn hunt in the elsewhere. midland county of Leicestershire.

(Eurobonds are bonds denominated in, say, dollars instead of euros. They migrated to London when New York introduced a tax in 1963 that in effect denied foreign investors access to US bond trading. As a result, all the major Wall Street banks set up subsidiaries in London where they have remained. London's 'light touch' regulation in the early 2000s again enabled them to do business forbidden to them in New York. Clemm is also remembered for not employing graduates who lacked experience of the wider world, perhaps because he had also been an anthropologist and had spent much time in Africa. He had also developed the floating rate note, which I do not intend to describe. There is now a graduate fellowship scheme in his name at Harvard and Oxford.)

Rumoured to file the biggest expenses in the banking business, von Clemm plainly found the lunch menu that day positively to his liking, albeit accidentally so. He was reminded how, in Boston, neglected wharves had been revived in the interests of commerce, as well as creating a pleasant environment. He was inspired to believe that Canary Wharf, despite its attraction for making fast food, could provide an even better recipe for his European offices.

It was clear that London would shortly become a world-leading financial centre, with a highly skilled workforce and relaxed regulations – even if these were regretted later.

Growing interest meant that the cost of space in the City of London was now astronomical compared with capital cities Canary Wharf would do just as well, with very much lower overheads. And escaping local taxes for the first ten years most certainly sharpened the corporate appetite. Von Clemm took the next Concord flight to New York, a trip he took on a regular basis, and contacted an expert in property development with the improbable name of Gooch Ware Travelstead, a big man from Kentucky, otherwise known (to Londoners) as Gee Whiz. He ran First Boston's property division.

Travelstead produced a plan, supported by Morgan Stanley and First Boston, for a financial centre to compete with the City right there in Canary Wharf. He wanted ten million square feet of space with 8.8 million square feet of offices for state of the art financial trading. He wanted half a million square feet for shops, plus two hotels with 800 rooms, plus parking for 11,000 cars. There would be twenty four separate buildings in all, but with three great towers in all, the highest anywhere in Europe. That was in 1984.

And so began the mass migration of financial and supporting business out of the City of London. There was a tightening of belts and a firming of lips and a brave pretence that none of this mattered, but this was probably the biggest threat to (what had been called) the City in its considerable lifetime. Now there was no doubt that the City of London was competing with a brash new neighbour by the name of Canary Wharf. But (surprise, surprise) London's second city was mainly in the borough of Tower Hamlets which very few outside of London's centre had any idea existed.

It did not happen quite as planned, for reasons that will be spelt out later, but the motivation had been created to get the circus on the road and it never stopped after that.

It did not take long for the City of London to react by relaxing rules on new Square Mile buildings. Michael Cassidy, chair of planning in the square mile, argued in favour of allowing 17m square feet of additional high-rise offices. By 1986 this had helped to cut the cost of space, and the development in Canary Wharf was hit by the competition. But an overall fall in the cost across London was welcomed by every tenant.

This general increase in commercial interest was all good news to the LDDC, which had the task of creating a framework to allow development to happen. It had the power to seize all land that was previously held by any state body and sell it off to any developer with the ability to make it work. It could also, compulsorily, buy the rest. It could use the income from selling this land in any way that would boost the area in any way it liked.

There was an annual grant passed down from government, to be added to the general pot and which varied in size from year to year, but which originally went to the heavy expense of clearing away the waste and providing essential services, as well as administration, of course. There were also funds for local government to reverse deprivation in urban areas. These were now taken from local councils and passed instead to the LDDC. Quite a considerable pot, in total.

Unlike normal planning permissions, none of this was subject to appeal. The Corporation's decision was final. As the Corporation was answerable only to government and the relevant minister, the only hope of stopping its progress was by direct appeal to Parliament. This was attempted more than once, but with limited success.

Back in 1981 the overall plan was to provide incentives enough to persuade private interests to invest even greater capital, to produce the maximum (hopefully a multiple) benefit. This should then produce extra income for the state in the form, over time, of taxation. It should also provide employment.

Heseltine had a friend, Nigel Broakes, a property developer who part owned The Ritz and the *Daily Express*, with the builder Lord Matthews who owned *The Financial Weekly*. Broakes accepted the job of LDDC chairman, with a Labour MP, Bob Mellish, as his deputy; you could see this, perhaps, as political insurance. The chief executive, Reg Ward, was appointed because of his experience of local government and of planning in particular.

I was one of the first generation of workers in the very first building to go up in Canary Wharf where I was editor of the monthly *VentureUK*. What had been a desert six months later saw an instant growth of lampposts and trees, many other buildings and parking restrictions comparable to any city centre. The godfather had made it happen. Mind you, that office building, which the LDDC said should be of good London brick, was later demolished, as their minds had been changed. However, as the LDDC paid compensation, the owner had no major gripe. He had enough in his back pocket by then to buy the *Daily Express*.

There was also, of course, a board of directors, originally only from the property sector, which was later extended to include a councillor from each of the affected local authorities: Tower Hamlets, Newham and Southwark. Greenwich and Lewisham were not invited, although originally planned to be part of the process, as somebody somehow changed their minds. Lord Heseltine has since told that me that he thought this was wrong; they should have been included.

But the board members from local authorities could hardly be seen as of much importance, no matter what skills they offered, as they were sworn to corporate secrecy. This meant that their representative role, their moral justification for joining, was totally overridden. In time this meant they would all step down and would only return with firmer conditions, clearly defining the benefits due to their individual boroughs. They said. But the trouble then was not much different. The agreements were reached with council leaders, with the moral support of their titular mayors, but were not revealed to their fellow councillors or members of the public. Secrecy reigned supreme still; just as today, commercial confidentiality had more muscle than democracy.

Now we have a lot more detail of what was agreed between the parties, but the fact that the public was kept in the dark did little to develop good public relations. The LDDC was experienced in the discipline. They spent millions of pounds every year on it, using the most expensive consultants. They also insisted that their deputy chairmen, an impressive series of good Labour lords, pressed the flesh at many public meetings, smiled broadly and shook many hands. Inevitably, local councillors seemed little more than lackeys by comparison.

Equally, when the LDDC board met, the business done was also secret. At least, no notes remain of the business. They may have been spending taxpayers' money, but they had no intention of saying how, apart from a summary annual statement. And the amounts involved were truly immense, as will be shown in later pages.

Perhaps the most important problem between the Corporation and local government was the standard process of planning permission. The LDDC was in charge of strategy, while local government was supposed to have the power to quibble on matters of detail. Defining the border could never be easy. But as the corporation had arranged the deal and was deeply involved with the project finance, such as granting credit and setting the price, sometimes much below market value, there was little chance for local councillors to insist on their normal building standards. This, after all, was the real world. In later years a committee was formed, including councillors, to handle planning, but in earlier years there was no committee. Often it was just the deputy chairman who decided yes or no.

It is also important to understand that although the official development area covered eight and half square miles of docklands, on both sides of the River Thames, the land that the LDDC controlled entirely on behalf of the public was less than half the total. The rest was owned by a mix of companies, both public and private, which the LDDC had to try to persuade to fall into line with the overall plan. Of course there were major tools on hand, mainly by providing infrastructure, but compulsion was not one of them.

Even with a planning committee, the various chief executives found that they had to seize every possible chance to move opposing opinion sideways. Oiling wheels, you could well call it, and many were oiled upstairs in The Grapes. This was the pub in Narrow Street, Limehouse, made famous by Charles Dickens in *Our Mutual Friend* as The Six Jolly Fellowship Porters. As a child, he also danced on the tables, so launching his dramatic skills.

And the corporation was never big. Heseltine had always thought that a core office was all that was needed, with major projects passed to consultants. His plan for a staff of 35 was argued up by the first CEO to something closer to 75, while the accounts have shown that employing consultants in fact cost more than employing staff. This was to lead to severe rebukes by auditors and politicians on the way that this was done. For the first five years there was no competition in employing consultants and, even after warnings, a quarter of contracts were still being issued in this personal, casual way. It was true that government approval was needed for any contract over £50,000, but a great many seemed to have been agreed at a convenient £49,999. Some consultants were former members of the staff of the LDDC.

For several years Dame Elizabeth Filkin, former head of the Citizens Advice Bureau and later the parliamentary commissioner for standards, assumed the LDDC role of revenue adjudicator, but it is not too clear what difference this made.

All power corrupts is a well-known phrase. But to what extent, in this case, was this true?

Michael von Clemm
Picture courtesy of Albert H Roux

THE LODGER
Promises

This is how Canary Wharf very nearly never happened, how it could have disappeared in a puff of dust. In *The godfather* chapter the tale is told of how the European chairman of Credit Suisse First Boston, Michael von Clemm, flew back to New York in 1984 to recruit the assistance of Gooch Ware Travelstead, then chairman of First Boston Real Estate. On the face of it, this seemed a smart move. Travelstead (in New York called Ware) had made a strong impression on the US bank, especially by producing income in a year when they were preparing to announce their very first loss. Thanks to him, they showed a profit.

The son of a builder from Baltimore, he was working as a consultant in a ski resort when he met people from the bank at a trade fair in Chicago. They thought he might be able to help with some lighting problems in their New York offices. He did. And within days he was shedding light on how the company could make big money by moving out of the financial district and Park Avenue. He negotiated a lease at below current rates with a $104m construction loan and sold the lease of the existing offices for a profit of $7m. Suddenly First Boston found they were out of the red and into the black, for which the president, Peter Buchanon, said the company was eternally grateful. That eternity was not to last.

It did not take long for Travelstead to persuade the bank to open a division for real estate, at the same time as financing him as a partner. They would share the deals and share the profits, which for the first few years were sizeable. One deal persuaded a Japanese company to pay the highest price ever for a New York office tower of $550 a square foot.

Travelstead adopted a life style appropriate to his situation; an apartment in Park Avenue, a mansion in Greenwich, a yacht and various luxury cars. He paid for people to holiday abroad, in Barbados, Sardinia and Venice. Not any people, you understand. Just those with loads of money who might return the favour.

There was no doubt that Travelstead had the quality golden touch. He walked the walk and talked the talk with the LDDC and government ministers. He even charmed Margaret Thatcher. He persuaded First Boston, Credit Suisse and Morgan Stanley to offer the finance to start the building. The impression he made in London at the time is still remembered remarkably clearly. Londoners were dazzled.

Two years later Morgan Stanley and Credit Swiss were not prepared to wait any longer. There was no cash coming in. You do not normally start on a project this big until you have some firm indication that tenants are committed. The list was pathetically small. Travelstead blamed the conservative British. He said they were scared by size. He should know. He was not only big and tall, but famous for his temper. His brother, Malcolm, would later explain that 'he was not a person who likes to be confronted'. Finally First Boston did a sideways deal with the Reichmann Brothers at Olympia and York in July 1987 to take the whole thing over.

It was not a total waste of time. Travelstead shared in the profits of the sale, plus fees, that left him considerably richer. This was said at the time to be near $8.5m, but later, under oath, he had to admit that it was 'just shy of $46m'.

Others who benefitted a great deal less included his business partner, Eduardo Canet, who had spent two years on the London deal and another two and half years on others. His salary was $100,000 a year, plus the promise of a share of the profits. This is what bankers call earning sweat equity. Eric Flounders, lead councillor of Tower Hamlets, and Brian Williams, then the mayor, were full of admiration for Canet's ability to make progress and get things done. He even stayed on with Olympia and York, to manage the change of control to them. Nine years later he was in a New York court claiming payment plus bonuses from Travelstead. Not an easy move, as both men and their wives had been close for a long time. But he won the case, in just one of many claims that finally closed down Travelstead.

It is inevitable in the building business that hard words are exchanged when projects fail, but Travelstead seemed to have a talent for attracting more than most. First Boston disowned him in 1988 after they had jointly bought 383 Madison Avenue, alongside the Grand Central terminal. It had cost them $80.5m in 1982, with the help of Arab money.

The 140 storey tower they planned for the site never saw the light of day, as a result of disagreements with the city over who had the right to do what. The battles in court cost tens of millions. First Boston were not amused.

In 1994 when Ware staged a Christmas party in Barcelona with Margaret Thatcher as a guest of honour to market some property, an investor was persuaded to pay $500,000, in the belief that Mrs Thatcher was also investing, jointly with Lord McAlpine, the Conservative party treasurer. The result was a major loss for the Japanese and US investors, who carried all the financial risk, followed by a criminal charge for fraud in Barcelona.

This was also painful for Eduardo Canet, who had championed the Barcelona project ahead of the 1992 Olympics and who had conducted all the detailed work there, if only, of course, because he spoke Spanish, which Ware did not. And he had to sue for his share of the equity.

Travelstead did liaise with Lord McAlpine, in buying a property company in Australia which had beach resorts that were deeply in debt, but the $3.8m of loans he raised and lost here were the absolute last straw. In no way could he could deliver.

Travelstead was described by Richard L Fisher, a major investor in New York property as 'The most fascinating person I have ever met. His visions were fantastic and almost always pure fantasy, destructive to all those around him.' Another former colleague, Raymond Velasquez, had a similar description: 'The most charming, intelligent individual. Of all the con men I have dealt with in my life, he is the most cunning and ruthless.'

Such was the man who might have been responsible for London's second city. Which means that Canary Wharf as we know it would probably never had happened.

THE BROTHERS
The Reichmanns

amuel Reichmann was a Jewish Hungarian merchant who fathered five sons after moving to Vienna in 1928, where he sold eggs on an international basis. Come the second world war they moved to Tangier, while two of the boys were schooled in England at the Gateshead Talmudical College. And Samuel started a bank. Then, in 1955, most of the family moved to Canada. They started a business importing tiles but, when they needed a bigger warehouse, they could not afford even the lowest quotation, so decided to try to build it themselves. What they learned, by managing it personally, was that the price they'd been quoted was in excess of costs by something in the region of eighty percent. What a really juicy profit! Just the business for them! It seems, as amateurs, they had built at lower cost and more skilfully than competitors.

Paul Reichmann, already qualified as a rabbi, became project leader of York Factory Developments Limited, formed with capital of C$40,000. His brother Albert was to later join him, as they climbed from project to project. Paul would be executive chairman, Albert would be president. York was the part of Toronto where they started. Now they were a band of three.

Olympia was a brand of men's socks they rather liked the sound of. Hence the new name of Olympia and York which was one day to make its mark in London by building Canada Wharf. In the thirty-odd years before Canada Wharf, Paul and Albert would build an empire in North America of amazing size. They would own about eight percent of New York. This was even more than the Rockefellers. They would also donate to mainly Jewish charities over $1bn in their flourishing years. In 1991 *Fortune* magazine said that the Reichmann family had by then become the fourth richest in the world.

If the Reichmanns had a charmed existence it could have been because of their strict adherence to Orthodox Jewish principles. All 613 of them. One product of this was their prohibition of any of their staff from working on the Sabbath, but also of any contractor. Not one brick was laid after sundown on any Friday. Another product was the value of their promise to deliver any building on time and on price. No matter what else might happen in the world, that promise was always kept, even if not confirmed in writing.

But their reputation was greater than that. Building a factory for themselves in Toronto persuaded them that the greatest efficiency was the real secret to making money. If there was a better system for doing anything, they were the first to know.

Certainly few others could know as much, as Olympia and York was a family company, unlisted on any stock exchange, so not compelled to publish its figures, which meant that doing business with it would always depend on trust. Paul was quiet and bearded, always dressed in black, and his Jewish skull cap gave the signal that here was a man of principle.

When it came to building Canary Wharf, the biggest project they had ever tried, they had already forgotten ladders and cranes. Keith Roberts, their English head of construction, despite advising against the project, persevered with a construction system they had tried and tested many times before, which was to use the lifts fitted out for the building to also move the construction materials. Some of them would be doubled-decked and able to carry impressive loads of 130 tons an hour. A turntable in the basement would move these loads between lift shafts according to need. Up inside the building they'd go, through one shaft or another. Faster building sped loan repayment, so seriously slicing the cost. At the core of it all was a book of instructions, that described the work systems in greatest detail and timed to the nearest minute. A Talmud of construction, even if not exactly orthodox.

The Reichmann plan for Canary Wharf was to slightly exceed the Travelstead vision. They would have ten million square feet of offices, 500,000 square feet of retail and 425,000 square feet of housing, but only 6,500 car spaces.

When Canary Wharf was bought from Travelstead in 1987 for £80m (on the advice of Charles Young of Citibank Canada) Reichmann declared he would not need to raise money as Olympia and York had an annual cash flow of $400m. Not true. Raising finance to put up buildings then became their newest skill. This was often done by getting a mortgage covering no more than half the value of any of their existing buildings. This would mean that the total building could hardly ever be put at risk. Other devices came along, such as exchanging shares with other developers. A favourite move was to get a bank that had provided the finance to move into the building, so cutting debt by the value of the rent.

And deals over prices were always done. Clearly, some tenants were more desirable, as their reputations were often the draw for less prominent tenants. So prices for better tenants were lower. For example, at Canary Wharf a fellow Canadian, Conrad Black, got an incentive of £20m for moving in his newspaper, *The Daily Telegraph*. That was something that most of the staff resented, especially the elderly Baron William Deedes, a friend of Mrs Thatcher. ('Come and rescue me, my boy' he would say in many a desperate phone call.) Later the paper, disputing the rent, would move to Westminster, by Victoria Station. By then Black had been jailed for fraud.

In the end, though, the financial games got the better of the master craftsmen. In 1991 they were running an empire of 165 companies, many apparently created for the purpose of transferring shares in actual assets. They had interests in oil and forest products and numerous bits of real estate, mainly in Britain, the US and Canada, but with branches in many more countries. It would seem that relying so much on finance to produce an income, instead of buildings, they were easily upset by a fall in demand for property in recession. Barely half of Canary Wharf had been sold, with nothing at all to British tenants. They could not repay their debts.

Owing more than $20bn, the company was put into administration, which is one remove from total collapse by passing control to a public official. This works differently in different countries. In the US and Canada the courts take over and supervise the existing company directors. The British system is less accommodating to existing management, with the courts appointing administrators, in this case PWC, who can then dismiss the existing directors. Here, that is exactly what they did. A holding company was formed, Sylvester Investments, chaired by Lord Levene. That was in 1992.

But Paul did not give up. With the help of George Soros, a fellow Hungarian, and the Saudi Prince Al Waleed, he raised $800m, enough to become chairman again. That was in 1995.

But ten years later the principal shareholders, determined to have their loans repaid, took total control of the development in Britain. Their holding company was Songbird Estates. By 2009, after fourteen more lean years, the main shareholders were the sovereign funds for Qatar and China and the New York based Simon Glick, who had been involved from the start. There is very little British investment. Canary Wharf is now fully let.

Recently Paul explained to a journalist that his religion had preventing him from gambling, but that property had been his compensation, his version of Las Vegas. The brothers, Canary Wharf behind them, after seventeen years of rock and roll, are now said to be looking for investments for their last $100,000.

Paul Reichmann

THE ENGAGEMENT
Interaction

For Canary Wharf, engaging with business and the public was key. But the way the godfather conducted business was quite unique in the history of Britain. Those largely unelected individuals, the directors of the LDDC, had access to hoards of public assets to a total value of about £2 billion. The way they used these was up to them, with the understanding that the final objective was to regenerate the docklands. (Was does regenerate mean? Good question. There was much disagreement on that.)

A number of chairmen and chief executives were in charge of this over seventeen years and the ride was easier for some than for others.

As an urban development corporation, the LDDC had a number of tools. These included planning permission without the fear of appeals from the public, an annual grant from central government, plus urban development grants that previously went to local government, the ability to seize land in its area for a price established by the district valuer, and the ability to resell that land to the highest or, possibly, the preferred bidder at what became the market price.

So the corporation became Britain's biggest player in the commercial and domestic property market. For instance, in its first seven years it acquired nearly 2,000 acres and sold on just 650, which left it with a useful land bank of 1350 acres.

It is hardly surprising that a shortage of supply at a time when demand was rapidly rising would at times increase values by a multiple of five once the LDDC took ownership. This seemed like blissfully easy money.

Clearly, this moved the corporation above the level of a local authority, passively restricted to granting permissions, and made it a major player in the market, with no need to take either the first or the highest offer, but with a certain ability to influence prices by controlling supply and demand. Even the technical lack of planning powers did not deter officers from expressing opinions on what they thought would be best in each case and from making sure that they got it.

On the other hand, to be quite fair, producing profit was not the whole picture. As any property developer knows, creating initial demand is hard. It is always best to create a trend by setting a good example. This means persuading a leading brand to move in ahead of others. The trouble is that the leading brand knows this and insists on getting a financial inducement to cover it (it will say) for risk, quite apart from major help with marketing. So the bargaining begins.

But urban development area status was not the only tool in the kit. Alongside creating the LDDC, the government also launched an enterprise zone in a centrally sited area. This was perhaps the most crucial key to getting business moving in the docklands. It promised ten years of relief from taxes, duty and employment training levies, as well as freedom from planning permission. It was certainly a sellers' market.

But the buyers were not totally helpless, especially if they had muscle. When the Canadian developers Olympia and York took over Canary Wharf in 1987 and announced their plans for Canada Tower, covering much of the enterprise zone within the urban development area, it was said that the world's biggest property developers had thus avoided £1.33bn in taxes in those crucial first ten years. (Their construction plans were different from Travelstead's, in planning first one tower, not three, then opting for 40, not 24 buildings, then halving the space for car parking.)

Further, the Reichmann brothers, the private company's three directors, exercised their power as brand leaders to negotiate the keenest price, paying the equivalent of £400,000 an acre, when the average in London was nearer £1m and when land on North Quay at the time had gone for £5m an acre.

Yet the Reichmanns offered much more in kind. So much to pay for environmental improvements. So much to help with investment in transport, like the DLR and the Jubilee Line, the extension of which to Canary Wharf was a condition they demanded. They even paid to push legislation for the new transport routes on its way through Parliament, some £2.5m for technical documentation, to be deducted from the purchase price of course.

It should also be said that the Reichmann brothers, with some years of experience of major projects, had finely honed and well-financed skills in community relations. When the LDDC was persuaded to pay much greater attention to local interests, they were following examples already set by Olympia and York. Sweeteners, inducements for the local population had already been distributed. The loss of all this was an added problem when a slump in the world-wide property market impelled this exceedingly private company into liquidation in 1992.

There was much space unsold in Canary Wharf. The company's debts world-wide were $20bn. The shock was apparently great for them, but no less so for the LDDC. Lord Heseltine was to say later that he felt partly responsible for the problem, by not ensuring that the local infrastructure, like roads and railways, had been in place in time to inspire more interest.

Despite their boasts, the Reichmann brothers did not provide finance entirely on their own. They were heavily in debt to various bankers, who had no choice but to assume ownership and try to carry on.

This, you might well say, is when the men took over from the boys. The Canary Wharf Group was then created, belonging to a brand new holding company called Sylvester Investments. The banks put in another £1.1bn and Lord Levene was put in charge, which looks quite normal when you think of his background. A close friend of Michael Heseltine, whom he advised for years on defence procurement, and a former Lord Mayor of the City of London, Levene had already sorted the faltering DLR when chairman. He had also become chairman of the challenged LDDC in 1991. Hence, the three most senior roles in this emerging city in the former docklands were all held by a single man. His earning power must have been considerable. Whatever it was, it is hard to resent it. The problems went away.

Two years later, much like a phoenix, Paul Reichmann, with the help of friends, offered and paid £800m to repurchase The Canary Wharf development from its accidental owners. A bargain in many more ways than one, especially when you think that three years later it was valued £1.4billion and four years afterwards *Forbes* magazine said it was probably worth $4billion. Mind you, as a private family company, a lot of this has to be guess work. Much as the LDDC's accounts were never that specific.

The fact that this massive and central development was the flagship of the development area made it important to the LDDC, apart from the involvement of Lord Levene for a crucial, shaky period.

Many people have pointed out that, although the LDDC was created to overcome inefficiencies in London local government, the LDDC in fact became a beast with problems of its own. The first CEO, Reg Ward, earned fame for his autocratic ways. There is little doubt that he attracted loyalty from those who were willing to fall for his charms, but others who cared more for principles were dismayed by his almost chaotic style. The first chief planner, Gordon Cullen, resigned when his careful rules on design and planning were swiftly abandoned in the face of what then was probably described as market forces. Others would mutter about politics.

Relations with funding government departments were also subject to Reg Ward's whims, as their obvious need to be kept informed on what was happening to public money was very seldom satisfied. The LDDC became reluctant to share information in any direction, with the government or the public.

Ward was finally persuaded to go in 1987 by Michael Portillo, then the relevant minister, in favour of a Major General Rougier, who lasted no more than 16 days, finding the behaviour of staff unregimented. There may have been a shortage of charm somewhere.

Next in post was Michael Honey, who was no doubt seen as a safe pair of hands, but whose four year tenure was marked by small progress, despite a lot of meetings and a deal of paper. One complication was the change of direction in favour of paying more attention to community relations as a result of pressure from a parliamentary committee. New staff were engaged and big promises made which, after the event, were not financially obvious. The £50m on offer was swift to disappear.

Finally, in 1991, the government lost patience with the cloudy thinking and imposed another CEO, Eric Sorensen, who had the advantage of having previously run the development corporation in Liverpool. Undeniably a more flexible man, he tidied things up ahead of closure of the

LDDC in 1998. Most important, he reversed the policy of pretending to be a civic body and tried to ensure, in the final days, a greater attention to infrastructure.

THE CELEBRATION
The big man

New York's Manhattan Island houses the World Financial Center. This was built by the Reichmann brothers' company Olympia and York, which also made possible Canary Wharf, often called Manhattan on Thames. Both also housed what are called winter gardens, essentially vast, glass covered structures designed for indoor social events. In London in the summer of 2011 one such event was a celebration to the memory of Reg Ward, the first chief executive of the LDDC, who had passed away some weeks before. It was a warm and touching event.

A video address by Michael Heseltine paid tribute to the work of Ward, including regret that 'the powers that be' had failed to recognise Ward's efforts in getting everything going. No MBE or CBE, as would have been normal for a senior civil servant with a solid record of service. Those present at the celebration, mainly former employees, sympathised with this observation. I saw no tears, but there was certainly sadness at what had seemed to be a slight to a man remembered as an inspiring leader.

However, there were also others in the room (although, naturally, clapping politely) who could also remember this CEO as a charming but very difficult person. Retirement before his task was finished had not been on his agenda. There were eleven more years to go.

However, there are leaders, plainly, who can manage best upwards, some who manage best downwards. Not many can manage both. Ward was clearly a downwards man. He knew what he wanted and was determined to get it and relied on his staff to handle the detail. He trusted them, made them feel important in everything they did. If they made mistakes, if he made mistakes, he would shrug it off and move right on. He was good at reading body language, not common among civil servants. The speed at which he worked was impressive. The optimism he showed was infectious. His finance director, Eddie Oliver, was equally skilful at creating the impression that everything was fine.

It did not hurt that the work in hand for these mostly local government people was highly original and greatly important to the future of the country. This was not some small town hall. The eyes of the world were upon them. The CEO had made it plain that what they did was important.

On the other hand, Ward happily described himself as a romantic dreamer with both feet firmly in mid air. Without doubt others would find this uncomfortable, especially those who ranked above him, and increasingly they said so.

There were vast amounts of public money being regularly passed to the LDDC from various government departments, from people with a culture of accountability. It was only reasonable, it seemed to them, for Ward to explain what he did with this money, and preferably offer his plans for approval. Ward did not see it that way. He knew, if he did that, it would be very hard for others not to interfere. This could lead to immeasurable delays and, possibly, lost deals. After all, Canary Wharf now had to compete with the City of London in attracting major clients. Instead, he took evasive action, being hard to reach, not answering calls, and committing the LDDC to deals ahead of consultation. In short, he ran this public agency very much like a private company, for the maximum effect.

Ward had taken some important initiatives. To have a light railway. To inspire an airport. To open the door to financial services. But, in the end, his principal backers no longer felt they had sufficient trust to leave him in control. The amount of public money at stake was growing exponentially. An organisation of this size and importance, now up and running fast, needed a safer pair of hands.

The sad reality is that anybody who annoys enough people in power over time is hardly likely to be rewarded for services to the crown.

Reg Ward

THE IN-LAWS
Pressure

Plan society as much as you like, for the better common good of all, and the probability is always high that someone will not want to join for one reason or another. That was certainly true on the Isle of Dogs during the growth of Canary Wharf. Again, this was almost a natural product of the culture of the area. Some councillors thought they had jobs for life, to work democratically for the people, with many returned to office in succession, but most, it seems, had overlooked the essential, very basic loyalty of East Enders to their neighbours. I have used the label in-laws for this chapter to describe those not directly responsible, but who are closely involved, so determined to get what they think is best.

Tenants of local council housing were especially used to working together and fighting hard against whoever for the services they needed. It was almost a full-time occupation for those without jobs and with little else to do. And when plans were announced for major changes, imposed by national organisations, uncertainty gradually grew.

Their defiance had a lot to do with losing trust in local politicians who were doing their best to negotiate terms. The willingness of local leaders even to talk to their national enemy was seen by locals as dodgy. This was especially felt by most, if not all Labour loyalists, as the national government was now Conservative. Surely the twain should never meet?

The result was that many local people formed themselves into pressure groups. There were said to be six hundred in 1983, including the Docklands Forum, the Joint Docklands Action Group, the Docklands Community Poster Project, the Docklands Consultative Committee, the Association of Island Communities, and so on. This did not say much for local politicians and their ability to represent. 'Kill the canary, save the island' was a slogan often used.

Some even looked for new politicians inside the fascist BNP, the British National Party, and they once elected a BNP councillor. Members of the Labour Party grew equally insecure. Some local groups could work together, some local groups just squabbled. When the strongest managed to make a difference the envious called them the mafia.

Sister Christine Frost and Rita Bentley were names (and voices) heard more often than most. Former councillor Peter Wade, an activist much liked by the media, was later persuaded to advise the Reichmanns in dealing with the remaining activists.

(All this was reflected in recent years when the notoriously disrespectful Scottish politician, George Galloway, persuaded malleable Bangladeshis to form a party he ironically called Respect, to claim seats on Tower Hamlets Council. This also faded fast, but not before delivering a healthy kicking to the political elite.)

But, earlier, the Isle of Dogs of Action Group had

succeeded in persuading the Greater London Council, then responsible for education, finally to open a badly needed school, for 1,200 children, all over eleven, who were forced to travel out of the area, despite the existence of available buildings. The George Green Comprehensive school was reopened in 1973. (George Green had made money in the nineteenth century building ships, so had paid for the original school.) Local borough politicians were conspicuous by their absence.

There was some confusion at public meetings that were called to discuss the development plans. Ken Livingstone, Labour leader of the GLC, with Labour councillors and MPs, had expected overwhelming support for their vehement opposition to it all and were plainly surprised when several residents said that development could be good.

Of course, there were flows between the pressure groups, as well as between the politicians, and the LDDC played whatever game it needed to get things done. Like employing protesters to work for them. Not that it really wanted to play: it had its own clear plans for progress and a reporting path directly to a minister who provided an annual income. In the early years it saw consultation as little more than public relations – in the worst possible sense of that phrase.

But the public row forced the corporation to appoint a community liaison officer in 1983, progressing to a director of community services in 1988, finally crowned by a code of consultation, agreed in 1990 - with councils, if not pressure groups. But this, of course, was a good nine years after the corporation began and a long time after Olympia and York had formed links of its own.

But better late than never. Perhaps.

THE UNCLES
Governments

The solution to success with Canary Wharf was, sadly, very obvious: just override democracy. Government by the people? What's that? Our elected local representatives (uncles) had already got used to being overruled. The reality is that for the past hundred years the balance of power between national and local has been sliding relentlessly upwards. Originally local was most important, for the obvious reason that local is personal. Then centralisation took the crown, with the seductive logic that coordination trumped petty competition. This was reflected in the use of taxes - and money always rules, of course.

Now most state income is collected centrally and dispersed, naturally with centralised conditions. That means that locally elected politicians have little power without national approval, which often means by a different party with different motivations. So who best speaks for us? There is a similar dominance of national media, which has come to condition the minds of everyone into believing that central control in Westminster is very right and proper. (The Prime Minister runs the country, doesn't he?) And so to Canary Wharf.

In this case the machine created to override East End democracy, the London Docklands Development Corporation, was the work, as we know, of Michael

Heseltine. Not a normal politician. As a minister he held several briefs, with defence as one and local government as another.

As a Conservative party member he had risen high, under Prime Minister Margaret Thatcher. But he started public life investing in property, before moving into specialist publishing, as chairman of a company that managed to survive through waves of financial challenges. He had certainly earned millions. Personally he had also survived despite the handicap of dyslexia that made reading and writing difficult. He overcame this in early life and ended with a higher than normal ability to remember, reason, account and comprehend, all of which were extremely useful in his brilliant career. (He was recently voted by civil servants as their most popular minister ever, for his 'willingness' to delegate.)

Finally turning against Margaret Thatcher in 1990 and making a bid to take her place, his star fell slightly in party politics, but hardly at all in public life, as he continued to promote the causes he believed in, one of which was local government.

After some time at the political top, he produced major papers for the Conservative Party on the organisation of local government, especially promoting elected mayors as way of developing stronger leadership, of which he had some experience.

This hardly suggests a person stealing power from people. But it might suggest the sort of person who dismisses detail and prefers decisions that quickly produce results - and profits.

With the benefit of historical memory, people who now approve of the decision to create the LDDC in 1981 include a number who, at the time, were sincere and vocal opponents. People, for instance, like Conor McAauley, who led in talks with the LDDC for the London Borough of Newham. He now admits that the way in which his Labour council resisted it was to some extent misguided. The benefit in terms of new housing, transport links and general prosperity are, now, conspicuously obvious. For instance, the council's new town hall, a gleaming palace of glass and white concrete overlooking City Airport and a vast expanse of gleaming water is superior to most such buildings in any place on earth.

Also, of course, the choice of Newham as a suitable site for the Olympic Games depended greatly on the improved environment, especially including the transport links, that would not have happened if Canary Wharf as a development had not happened.

But the fact remains that the local councillors in the three boroughs affected by the plan were fiercely determined at the start of it all to resist as hard as possible. If only because they were Labour people and the national government, imposing the plan, was undoubtedly Conservative. So the councillors of Newham, Tower Hamlets and Southwark were at first reluctant even to talk with officials of the LDDC. (Lewisham and Greenwich, which had earlier belonged to the docklands collective, had by then been dropped.)

Not many people regretted this, if only because it was not too clear locally who was responsible for which part of government. The LDDC had a very broad brief to encourage development in its area, which included permission to put up buildings, but local governments retained their power to influence planning detail. Also councillors kept their powers to approve road building and alterations, which meant that they could, if they really wanted, close access to Canary Wharf. What they actually did in 1982 was to withdraw their delegates from the LDDC and stick their heads very firmly in the sand. Work carried on without them.

Four years later there was a major sea change, for purely political reasons. Since the Social Democratic Party was launched in Limehouse in 1981 by four former top members of the Labour Party (fighting elections with the local Liberal Party in 1983 and 1987, finally to merge in 1988), traditional patterns of party loyalty had increasingly started to shift. Most members of the Liberal Party had been born in other parts of Britain and many had arrived with good degrees from leading universities. They were also in their early thirties.

The change was strong enough in Tower Hamlets for, first, Liberal delegates to win elections, and then, in 1986, to take majority control of the borough for two elections running. What became the Liberal Democratic Party made an impression on local life that is still with us today? The East End had woken up, at least to living in the present and, hopefully, in the future.

Meanwhile, in 1990, the Thatcher government decided to centralise income from business rates, with Whitehall dispensing the income locally according to national plans. Democracy redefined again. In the context of Canary Wharf, the new local government saw its chance to benefit from the opportunity of introducing major improvements with the use of this centralised money. An early decision was to offer a delegate to join the board of the LDDC. Then, by agreeing to improve the access to the development by opening roads, they could bargain for benefits in kind. Compensation for moving housing, recompense by accepting payment for new homes built elsewhere.

Conversations also began with the people now building Canary Wharf. The Reichmann brothers at Olympia and York had a track record across the Atlantic of dealing tactfully with local people. On top of that, they had the benefit of the personal skills of Eduard Canet, who had handled such things for Gooch Ware Travelstead, the original developer.

Eric Flounders and Brian Williams, then leader and mayor of Tower Hamlets, are still full of praise for Canet's skills. He was the man who could get things done. Such as funding an educational trust. Such as setting up a construction college. Such as rejuvenating a housing estate. Such as helping to ensure that Canary Wharf would not become a gated community, which had always been the original aim, but instead would be open to the public. To a large extent, Olympia and York were taking initiatives that only later would occur to the LDDC.

Flounders and Williams remember the sweat of almost continuous evening meetings. They both had day jobs, if only because they only got expenses for their council work. (Not until 1995 did John Major's government agree to allowances for political leaders of local government and not until 2003 were councillors offered pensions. Now some council leaders are paid more than £70,000 a year.)

Flounders and Williams are understandably proud of the effect they had had on local government. As comparatively young men then, in their thirties, not even born in the area, they were determined to shake the borough up, to push it into the modern age. They still have copies of their television appearances, boldly explaining to the world at large just how the East End was going to change. Even they, though, were quite surprised at exactly how much it did change. Local people had been plainly miffed at how the established politicians had not even bothered to ask for their votes. Therefore they did not get them.

The example set then spread. A year after Tower Hamlets agreed to talk business with the LDDC, the borough of Newham fell into line, clearly aware that they could miss out on major financial inputs. However, Southwark decided to stand firm, so the LDDC invites former councillors to speak for the borough instead. That was in 1987. Finally a code of consultation with all boroughs was agreed in 1990, after which councillors joined the planning committee. About then Canada Tower was completed. Rather late for consultation, perhaps.

There is a complicated tail to this story. The Liberals, in their determination to boldly reshape Tower Hamlets, divided the borough up into areas. Each had its mini-council, each its own town hall. The idea of this, in effect, was to separate the Liberal strong north from the Labour strong south, so that each could go their separate ways without arguing with each other.

The LDDC found this very confusing. It was not sure who to deal with. The Audit Commission was then called in to describe it as a waste of money and demand a return to normal practice. In other words, just one town hall. Meanwhile Canary Wharf continued on its way.

While local councillors can clearly be seen to have made a certain contribution, it is none too clear who was taking the lead, who was making the big decisions.

Eric Flounders

PROCREATION
Transport

J ust as in birth, nothing really happens until the seed can reach the egg. Hence the slogan for Canary Wharf was always 'so near and yet so far', certainly in the early years. There had never been much need for transport. The people who lived and worked on the island had seldom sought to go elsewhere, while the cargo moving in and out could manage well with barges and lorries and, to move shipping coke, the occasional train. Close as it was to the City of London, which managed the commerce supporting the trade, the personal contact between the two was occasional and slight. Not ideal for a new, modern city where personal and instant communication is crucial to success.

Road, rail, air and water were the obvious options for personal travel. The first to be explored was rail. Reg Ward, first CEO of the LDDC, with his personal assistant Stuart Innes, set off round the world and returned to docklands with great enthusiasm for a light transport system. It became internationally known as the Vancouver Sky train, by the Canadian company Bombardier, which was originally known for snowmobiles. (No problems with the wrong kind of snow, then.) This was not an underground system, but ran on rails above the ground and, most important, was remotely controlled, a fully computerised programme. The budget was

£33m. Vancouver started in 1982, the same year as the DLR, but the Canadian version was entirely new, while the DLR depended on a network from a previous age, at least from the start.

The inherited network was for open trucks delivering coke for steam driven ships. But the new rolling stock was built for passengers, with roofs and seats and modern machinery and cars that were longer and heavier than trucks. The bends on the track were now too sharp, the bridges were not sufficiently strong and far too often the cars fell off. It only got worse with time.

For four years London Transport strove to make it work, but concluded in 1991 that the DLR should be closed for improvement. They thought this would take a year. The fleet of 11 cars were sold and replaced by a set of 70 new cars, with doors better equipped for the slightly more risky extension under the Thames to Greenwich. Everyone with money in Canary Wharf reacted with alarm, of course.

A special bus service had already begun, linking Canary Wharf to Mile End tube, on the District and the Central Lines. A bumpy box on four wheels, ambitiously named the Docklands Clipper, had run since 1984 but, apart from the cumbersome need to change transport, the congested roads over even that distance made travelling times uncertain. Weekly passengers grew from five to twelve thousand with an increasing number of buses an hour, right up until the start of the DLR. People did get to work, eventually, but the area's workforce had grown to a size that meant that better provision was crucial. Boats had also been tried for a while but, again, if you were not close to the Thames for both ends of your twice daily journey there were complications, walks and queues. And boats were never cost effective. Olympia and York met most of the losses until it seemed ridiculous.

Immediate action was badly needed to address the problem of commuter traffic and it was becoming obvious that the DLR management were just not up to the job. The cars were seriously overloaded. The suspicion was that the responsibility for running the very large, old London network had always got most of London Transport's attention, with the DLR seen as marginal.

Michael Heseltine's friend, Lord Peter Levene, with a reputation for solving such problems, was persuaded to grasp the nettle. His solution was to appoint a contractor to take sole control without halting the service, so taking it away from London Transport while passing supervision to the LDDC, where Levene was also chairman. The original spend of £77m was increased by a further £400m, to get it back on the rails, so to speak.

Even then there were still some problems. London Transport had refused to accept that the signalling system being used in Canada was suitable for London. The word tradition was used, I believe. But for two years from 1994 the Canadian system was slowly phased in, which led to delays and some weekend closures, but finally ended with a system able to locate the actual position of trains, which prompted a much more frequent service, as well, surely, as a safer one.

In 1997 the DLR was leased by the LDDC to a consortium of managers. In 2001 it was returned once more, in better shape, to London Transport. Now it provides, not a high speed system, but a definitely gracious form of transport, snaking its way between high buildings, many of them in glass and marble, and edging up and down the slopes, granting a range of panoramic views of water, land, old churches and trees. It is very popular with tourists.

A second type of train was more conventional: the tube, the London Underground. One reason for London Transport not giving DLR its full attention had been because the management was engaged with what it thought were bigger problems. There were plans for new lines all over. One of these had been around for years and was called the Fleet line, then the River line, and in 1977 was renamed Jubilee, to mark the 25th anniversary of the Queen assuming the throne.

The likely route had changed many times, partly depending on the forecast need and partly depending on available finance. However, it was clear that in reaching Canary Wharf from Waterloo, twice going under the Thames, it could carry three times as many commuters as already used the DLR. The commercial advantage to the City Mark Two was overwhelmingly obvious. The total cost was £1bn, with Olympia and York agreeing to put in £400m.

The line might never have passed through North Greenwich if British Gas, which owned the land there (the home of The Millennium Dome, now the O2), had not offered £25m. A Swedish house builder working north of the Thames was also approached for a contribution, but would not pay any more than that. So the line went under the Thames again.

In any case, Olympia and York had insisted to the LDDC that they could not start without the certainty of this essential piece of infrastructure. To that extent, they provided finance to create and speed the legislation through both of the houses of Parliament.

So now the area to the east of London has seen an explosion of railway routes not seen in any similar period. A look at the map will show: the silver coloured Jubilee line, from Stanmore to Stratford; and the double blue line, for the Docklands Light Railway, which runs from the Bank to Woolwich and Lewisham, all via Canary Wharf; and the double orange line which is cutely called the Overground, but which actually extends the East London line from Dalston under the Thames to Croydon. Soon you will be able to ride from Paris and Brussels by train to Stratford International, there to be joined by the Crossrail link from Maidenhead to Shenfield. The Crossrail station should open in 2017, costing £500m, with the Canary Wharf Group paying £150m of that. It is true that everything came in late, but now it is up and running.

Road access was a much bigger problem. The docks had been built to make movement difficult, to prevent the theft of unloaded cargo. And the roads that existed were built when transport was mainly by horse and cart. Making plans to improve road access had long been prevented by lack of agreement between a range of local authorities in charge of neighbouring areas. At least the LDDC could act in its own area without consultation.

The enterprise zone was the first to benefit, with a new road, Marsh Wall, costing £2.5million and called the Red Brick Road because of the paving, although the bricks were actually made of concrete. More access roads were built once the Labour Party lost control of Tower Hamlets and the Liberal Democrats, who took control, named their price for agreeing. The Docklands Highway, the Limehouse Link and the East India Dock Link to the A13 were all the subject of special agreements involving major compensation, in capital or kind.

The Limehouse Link had the doubtful distinction of being the most expensive piece of road ever built in Europe, if not the world. The problems of driving it through a tunnel and moving a large amount of housing, while compensating the people they moved, saw the estimated cost explode from an agreed £141.5m, to £227.6m at the start, to £448.6m at the finish. Seen another way, this put the cost at £4,500 an inch.

The British contractors had to be removed and replaced by Bechtel from the USA - not a very good example. Increasing the problem was the popular perception that the mainly Bangladeshi population who were made to move were then re-housed in former luxury accommodation in

Millwall. Political voices said this was favouritism. A lot less noticed was the offer on the table from Olympia and York to build the road at a much lower price. By then it was all too late.

In 1990 the Minister for Transport said he had already spent or reserved £3billion for investment in the area. £1.2billion of that was for roads outside of the LDDC space, improving wider access. That was the year when the Canary Wharf tower was formally opened for business.

A major gap that has still to be filled in the wider transport planning area is for a river crossing between Thamesmead and Beckton, nominally called the Thames Gateway Bridge. Either that or cable cars, as they have in Singapore. This has been considered for many years, with a great deal spent on outline planning and talk of creating 25,000 new jobs. The mayor of greater London rejected a second plan for a bridge in 2008, not just because of the £450m cost, but also because of lobbyists who insisted it would hinder, not help, real local ambitions. Planning the Olympics became more important.

After road and rail, the third major plank for transport links with Canary Wharf required no finance from the public purse, other than the allocation of land. This was London City Airport. In September 1981 the first CEO of the LDDC, Reg Ward, was invited to lunch by Philip Beck, then chairman of Mowlem, the builders. At the lunch was Bill Bryman, who flew small planes out of Plymouth Airport. The proposal was for a similar airport to Plymouth for flights from Canary Wharf. Bryman and Mowlem would finance it all, on the understanding that Ward would push for better land transport connections.

Six years later the business began, but changed hands a couple of times before sufficient flights and enough passengers provided a suitable income.

Local resistance did not help. Conor McAuley, a Newham councillor, remembers demonstrating at the airport when bigger jet planes were due to be used, replacing the small but quiet prop aircraft. To his surprise, once the planes had landed, he had to admit that the feared noise problem was nearly non-existent. Most locals, in fact, believed that the airport would provide good jobs where jobs were needed, so were largely sympathetic.

I was personally pleased when discovering that moving from Bow to Lille took just one hour, which is less than it takes to reach any other airport in England, quite apart from France.

The fact that the airport had no state finance was slightly ironic in the light of the fact that Canary Wharf was mainly dependent on foreign money. Michael Heseltine has also stressed that the O2 Dome and the new Stratford shopping centre, as well as the Excel exhibition area were all, also, foreign funded. And without so many foreign companies choosing London to run their international business nothing would have happened in the first place. So if the state had helped these people to visit without long treks from Heathrow or Stansted it would have seemed a sensible move.

Never mind, it happened through private investment.
Procreation has clearly begun.

Peter Levene

APPEARANCES
Architecture

For those who do not need to be there, Canary Wharf is just a group of buildings, effectively London's second city. They may visit it to shop or eat, but its appearance is what matters most, especially because it is so very different from much of the rest of London. And that is what they will talk about most. They either love it or hate it.

Somebody who said he hated it was the architect Sir Richard Rogers, who described it as a hymn to greed. Supporting him, from a different direction, was our conscientious Prince of Wales. He said that Londoners had already suffered enough from towers of architectural arrogance and that the development showed the triumph of commercial expediency over civic values. Also its railway, the DLR, was suitable only for Toy Town. He produced a very expensive book with illustrations by Canaletto to make the point that London before was similar to Venice. And now?

Venice, of course, was certainly mentioned when Canary Wharf was originally planned, asserting that the stretches of water were an inspirational force. Not only the Thames was close at hand, but also the many docks. But while it is obvious now that the docks have been used to flatter many buildings, London's mighty heart of a river has largely been ignored. Yes, river walks have been opened up, which before were blocked by industrial buildings, but not in a way to create an effect of drama or delight.

Even those docks still filled with water can lend only some of the Venice effect. An early advertisement to attract business tenants used the slogan: 'It will feel like Venice and perform like New York'. Well (overlooking aromatic canals), most visitors to Venice do not say they feel it, although they clearly adore its looks. And adorable anyway is not a word appropriate to Canary Wharf. A contemporary Venetian architect, Francesco da Mosta, has described towers as both beautiful and terrifying. Canary Wharf has many towers.

Venice, by the way, used a complex democracy which would have horrified the centralised LDDC, not to mention the City of London and the councillors of Tower Hamlets.

Two docks were filled in before the LDDC started, the London Docks at Wapping and the Surrey Dock in Southwark. Others have seen adjacent buildings overlapping at the edges. Michael Heseltine, after much had gone up, severely regretted the shortage of trees; not surprising from someone who has spent many years developing an arboretum.

This does not mean that there are no trees. Several hundred have been installed, but very largely in narrow strips, as a kind of cosmetic trimming. Beckton has the only real park, technically in the urban development area, but far from Canary Wharf. This compares with cities like Helsinki, where 30 percent of the urban space is green. The World Health Organisation believes that every individual needs 16 square metres of green space.

Of course there are plans to redress the balance, with 20 acres of landscaped parks, as and when the new building begins. And it is said that Canary Wharf can claim one of the highest concentrations of 'green' roofs, employing Sedum moss. That is not obvious from the ground, of course.

That the built environment affects our character is pretty obvious. Architecture, after all, is urban landscape. This does not refer to specific buildings, so much as their arrangement. There are various ways of handling this. One you could call the European, which tends towards co-ordination, which in turn calls for a certain amount of agreement and, usually, central planning. The result can then be called formal. Regular if predictable. Then there is the laissez-faire approach, which encourages individual freedom. Central planning is almost invisible. The result of this can then be called assertive, full of apparent energy.

After the Great Fire of London, Christopher Wren and other architects tried hard to use the opportunity to introduce a degree of formality, much as they have in Paris. He wanted to place the major churches at either end of newly built streets, to create a visual focus. The land owners, on the other hand, preferred to keep control of their property and lobbied successfully to do that. Hence we have, all over London, a generally mixed architectural economy. This was repeated in Canary Wharf, but for slightly different reasons. Here most land became the property, at least in effect, of the LDDC, but the brief was to sell it on for development as rapidly as possible. Flexibility was the key.

When the LDDC was launched it made brave plans to lay down rules. A design guide was commissioned in 1981. Later, in 1988, a similar master plan was ordered to develop Heron Quays. Very little if any of this has survived, which caused the chief architect and planner, Ted Hollamby to leave the corporation in 1985, no doubt with some chagrin.

But the economic pressures were strong. Some describe it as a battle that was won by the boardroom against the town hall. Hence there were no plans at the start at the project for training facilities, health or education, and very little for social housing. There were no civic squares or public buildings and certainly no parks. And the end result was strangely incoherent, with an uncoordinated number of buildings abruptly discontinuous in scale (a quotation from Brian Edwards in his excellent survey, *London Docklands*.) There was no landscape design, no grid of streets, while the walkways, of which there are many, appear to be only for private use, as they often suddenly come to an end. Street signs are largely invisible, so navigation is only possible with a random collection of guides.

Pressure from former Tower Hamlets councillors to keep the streets always open to the public can now be seen to have finally worked , but possibly too late. Unlike the City of London, Canary Wharf has a very strong feeling of insular indifference. If you have not been invited, do not come in, is the general impression. Summer concerts and winter ice skating are gestures of friendship towards the natives, but in a pre-ordained and formal way. They are no substitute for theatres and cinemas and buildings with open arms, so to speak. Of course there are a number of restaurants and pubs, but the setting for these elsewhere in the East End is usually more relaxed.

On the other hand, for those who are happy to wander around with no destination, the result can be exciting. The variety of shapes and sizes of building can seldom be predicted. The sequence seems haphazard. The discovery of very odd bits of architecture, with no apparent reason for existence, can equally well confuse or dismay. High quality finish on many buildings, with vast expanses of gleaming marble, certainly impresses, but only with ostentation. It is, to quote Brian Edwards again, like a museum of the environment.

In so far as most of the investment in Canary Wharf is from non-British interests, it is not surprising that, with so few controls, they would opt for architectural themes which are comfortable for them. American, Swedish, Japanese. These are influences easily found side by side. But this is not new to the whole of London. Foreign investment, financial and otherwise, is what has kept the place alive for centuries in the past.

The first CEO of the LDDC, Reg Ward, was the central judge on what was acceptable or appropriate for the second city, and his taste was shaped by his personal experience, for instance, of touring the USA before the LDDC began. He was wowed by the sheets of reflective glass which were then the latest innovation for office blocks in north America, so

City Airport, among other buildings, was going to have them too.

Central to Canary Wharf, of course, is the first tower block put up in the area, officially Number One Canada Place, designed by the Argentinean/US architect Cesar Pelli. Clad in gleaming British steel, the proportions suggest the Westminster Clock Tower, home of Big Ben, according to Pelli. Believe that if you will. For a long time it stood alone but, once the office market picked up, it developed some very close relations, albeit of varying quality.

Of course, underneath, in the Canadian manner, are terraces of shops and stores, carefully shielded from freezing snow, as and when it decides to fall in London. These took a very long time to arrive. Nine full (or empty) years, in fact. Retailers needed a lot of persuasion before they believed there was business to be done. The incomplete transport links did not help. There seemed little profit in office workers alone. What they needed was passing trade.

On the edges of the LDDC area, supermarkets had shown interest early: next to Mudchute Park on the Isle of Dogs, next to Greenland Dock in Rotherhithe, as well as in a shopping centre in Beckton. This is because they lay quite close to already existing housing. But right at the heart of Canary Wharf there were acres of empty spaces.

Lord Levene, who then chaired the development, told me that he pressed the flesh of many chairmen of major retailers, playing them off against each other, until finally he got a brand leader to commit to taking space. That was the chairman of Tesco. Other shopkeepers then felt more secure, with other brand leaders, such as Boots and John Lewis agreeing to take space as well. Most of the country's biggest retailers have opened branches in Canary Wharf shopping malls. And now, says Levene, the business is so good that customers often don't ask about price, only about delivery. Quick service food counters serving steak and champagne are used to £50 tips from traders who are pleased at being swiftly served on their twenty minute breaks.

Real East Enders are still not obvious, any more than are mothers and children, but there is no denying that there is real activity and business being done.

NO PLACE LIKE HOME
Housing

Yes, people live here, too, but how? Civilisation comes from the old word for citizen. Civis. It is no secret to say that cities are seen as places where people both live and work. Canary Wharf was different. Right from the start the project was planned primarily as a commercial venture. Which did not mean just that it had to make a profit, but it did mean that commercial tenants were the ones that mainly mattered. There is little doubt that this resulted in a less than civilised city.

The priorities were understandable. The desert called the Isle of Dogs had preoccupied years of local politics with plans to provide more homes for the homeless in what is now called social housing. Local politicians thought that winning votes depended on just that. The trouble was that nobody had found a way of raising money to do it. Certainly those in national government, usually expected to provide the cash, saw little point in pouring money over people who could neither work nor pay taxes. Hence a development plan was preferred that prioritised commercial growth to produce income for the greater good in a variety of ways.

We already know what happened then. Incentives were created to attract small companies, to create employment and, at some time, pay taxes, to be overwhelmed by giant companies in the business of moving money. The Big Bang had arrived in Britain and discovered Canary Wharf.

Local politicians found that much of their powers (such as they were) were taken away and given to the LDDC. This had nothing to do with democracy. It was simply the most convenient way of driving the programme forward.

Civilisation found it had a new meaning: government by civil servants. Also these eight square miles became the biggest building lot in Britain

Meanwhile, locals had little choice but to gaze, slack-jawed, at the relentless progress. Their community had been subsumed by men in suits from goodness knows where, determined to build a world on the place to carry out business of the kind of which the locals were totally ignorant. Imagine a person taking over your garden and installing, say, a machine designed to turn white mice into rabbits. It made just as much sense as that. And meanwhile (the important issue) people still needed places to live. The world was going crazy, wasn't it?

Of course, the subtext behind the plan was to overcome a dependency culture, where people believed they have a right to housing primarily paid for by others, usually at a price very far below what those others must pay for themselves. So the hope was that if jobs were created that paid well enough to inspire independence, then the whole idea of social housing would gradually fade away. Then everyone would feel better. Perhaps.

The reality was that families who found themselves lodged firmly at the bottom of the ladder could not so swiftly improve themselves. Every time a new child arrived, the budget went back down. Self-improvement also needs education, and educational provision then was not exactly excellent. With parents themselves little more than literate, their children had far to go.

In 1981, owner occupation in the area was far below the London average. Greater London averaged 49 percent, inner London 27 percent. But in Southwark it was 2 percent, in Tower Hamlets 3 percent, and 13 percent in Newham. New homes built locally in the previous five years were 83 percent council owned, compared with 31 percent in greater London. The local culture of social dependency was not getting any healthier.

Nevertheless, the LDDC to start with was focused mainly on attracting business and not until some time had passed was any thought applied to housing. And the godfather, the LDDC, had only outline planning powers, unlike normal planning authorities such as local borough councils. It also owned less than half the land for which it had overall planning control. So, once again, persuasion was the key, with the important lever of being able to provide the all-essential infrastructure.

The first chairman, Nigel Broakes, insisted to a committee of the House of Lords that his aim was for all new homes in the area to be divided in a rational way: 50 percent for owner occupiers, 25 percent for housing associations, and 25 percent for shared equity schemes. He was working to a development plan drawn up by accountants PWC. When the LDDC closed in 1998 some 24,000 new homes had been built, with 17,800 wholly owned, plus 6,250 in shared equity, and with 4,800 council homes (some 80 percent of the total) improved with LDDC finance. The target was almost met, you could say.

(Council housing, by the way, was largely moved to free-standing associations during the Margaret Thatcher government with the bright idea that this would shift more debt away from the government's books, so improving the look of the national economy.)

By this stage the resident population numbered 83,000. Gossip said that most of these were people you ought to heave 'alf a brick at, as they came from out of the area. In fact this was not entirely true. In 1989 45 percent of residents were of local origin, a year later 58 percent were. No doubt a lot of Canary Wharf workers, approaching 100,000 in 2009, were commuting in from other areas, bringing skills essential to the financial sector, but most of those who lived there were not greatly different from those who were there before. Whether this was good or bad, the reader must decide. But 24,000 new homes were built and the resident population doubled. Prices also more than doubled, which made affordable homes less possible, but perhaps most of the need had been met.

Yet credit must be given to the LDDC, together with those local councillors who finally agreed to join the committees formed to design the policies. Janet Ludlow, the Liberal from Tower Hamlets, is comfortable with knowing that she made a difference in favour of her electorate. No doubt the bargain with the Limehouse Link, the motorway needed to access the area which meant re-housing of hundreds of mainly Bangladeshi tenants in largely new up-market homes in Limehouse, created a degree of ethnic tension and for a while encouraged the British National Party. But all the same it attracted an extra £70m of subsidy and allowed the scheme to happen. It was complicated by many of the original homes being found to house more than a single family, thus making the move more complicated. Nearly one in five, in fact. Yet Canary Wharf without main road access is difficult to conceive.

But, politics aside, the major product of housing in the development area must surely be the wealth of architecture, in its variety and range. Nowhere else in greater London, largely famous for endless rows of identical ticky-tacky boxes, semi-detached and pebble-dashed, is there such a demonstratable wealth of personal identity. This is possibly due to the magnetic attraction of a major development being launched in a metropolis. Property companies from many countries made serious bids for pieces of land. On top of that, many local people decided they ought to do their bit in the form of self-build housing. The fact that some of these were builders gave the lie to the misconception that the locals lacked good skills.

Housing styles from Sweden and the Netherlands are interspersed with more conservative variations on English themes from various generations. Nautical symbols, as with office blocks, were scattered across the land. Comparing these with mid-Atlantic plays on styles of office development common to the Canary Wharf estate introduces a unique environment not seen in other cities. Convention is not a useful word. Result is surely what matters.

The process by which it all happened is something that needs to be known and considered. Property companies were just as shy of investing in housing as they were in offices when the LDDC began in business. They had to be induced. First of all, the LDDC reclaimed much of the docklands area. It had been the target for tons of rubbish, and most of it highly toxic. For many years afterwards the methane levels created record sickness rates in London. And early on the facilities were minimal. Very poor transport, very poor retail, little medical help, poor schools, and so on. But the incentives provided were tempting.

First, the developers could take the land and not pay for it until they'd sold housing. They had two years to do the deal. The only catch was that they had to provide some 40 percent of these homes at prices which were mutually agreed to be 'affordable', and that local people had to have first dibs. At the same time, interested local people were offered £10,000 of free loans towards their mortgages by the LDDC, which usually meant that each home was being subsidised by roughly £16,000. Six hundred homes in Beckton went in little more than a hundred days.

After that came Surrey Docks, with 480 homes. Then Wapping, on the site of the filled-in London docks. The

LDDC added extra value in the form of landscapes, roads and services. There was no shortage of demand. In fact, there were said to be many people who could claim to be locals one way or another, and so could bid for property at the head of the queue, but whose only intention was to sell and move on once property prices, as they did, improved. The LDDC knew that this was happening, and tried to prevent it with penalty clauses, but without a lot of success.

If there was any debate on housing quality, it has not survived the LDDC. New standards have been introduced in London that says that the minimum size for a house with three bedrooms is 1033 square feet. The Royal Institute of British Architects says that one third of new houses will not pass the test. Even at a two thirds success rate, this is hardly generous. The average French home is one and a half times bigger. The average home in the US and Australia is more than twice as big. Few homes in Canary Wharf compare.

The biggest challenge to the housing market arrived in 1988 with the end of the double mortgage interest relief and the general collapse of the housing market. The LDDC's revenue from land sales, a major form of revenue, fell from an expected £130m to an actual £10m in a year. The LDDC had to think again. It was at this time that the government provided the additional £70m.

But social housing seemed to flourish, despite the stress on private sales. A witness to this was Mike Tyrrell, who took over Tower Hamlets Community Housing after being deputy head of council housing for the whole Isle of Dogs.

He remembered deals made upstairs in The Grapes, the pub since bought by the actor Sir Ian McKellen from the former *Playboy* Bunny Girl Barbara Haigh with the help of the publisher Evgeny Lebedev. Tyrrell encouraged his older tenants to cherish their past in the old East End, as in reminding them of their summer holidays picking hops for beer in the fields of Kent. Now they have a beer of their own, produced from their very own hops.

There were many claims to be first with everything. Such as building London's first urban village by the Royal Docks at West Silvertown. Prince Charles thought this a good idea. Others remembered the former Poplar mayor, George Lansbury, having already done this, with the Chapel House Estate in 1920. He also insisted on the planting of fruit trees, even if most have now disappeared.

The best ideas are seldom new.

THE CHILD MINDER
Canary Wharf Group

anary Wharf is a flourishing child, but all the same it needs much care to guide its future growth. Those who gave it birth have largely moved on or have had other, more pressing, calls for attention. Lord Heseltine visits from time to time, anxious to encourage a bit more greenery, which is no doubt why, if the plan goes ahead to build another new town to the east, it will then have a park, a new canal and, impressively, an open high street.

Planning permission was won in 2008 from a supportive Tower Hamlets Council to replace what is known as Lovegrove Walk by South Dock by an 8.5m square foot development, probably to be called Wood Wharf, with office space and 1,600 homes, with a hotel, cafes and restaurants. The ground work has already begun. The council will gain by £24m for the upgrade of local amenities, while a separate £15m will be offered to the budgets for education and health. Meanwhile, the Canary Wharf Group is continuing to fund a Crossrail station, improvements to the DLR and services for buses. Movement depends a lot on the market, but it is a busy, busy time.

The person in charge of planning all this is little known outside of his office but has (surprisingly) been here since Olympia and York arrived in 1987. He is George Iacobescu, CBE. Dark featured and quietly spoken, he left his native

Romania in 1975 when dictatorship was at its worst. With French as his single alternative language, he chose to move to Montreal, in Canada. He had a soviet era academic degree from Bucharest University, in construction and engineering, but thought he should double check his credentials at Montreal University. Technically, he found he had nothing to learn.

Commercially, though, there was much to learn. Unlike in communist dictatorships, getting work in the western world depended less on corrupt officials and very much more on competitive skills allied to commercial reputations created in an open market. He found such skills in a business in Toronto, which partly attracted because its owners were also immigrants from central Europe, the Reichmann brothers at Olympia and York. He became line manager for the development and construction of Olympia and York's flagship in New York, the 8m square foot, waterside, World Financial Center. He also took care of the Olympia Center and the Neiman Marcus buildings in Chicago. He had clearly learned about business quickly. He had also mastered English.

When the Reichmann brothers opened shop in London in 1987, Iacobescu became Senior Vice President, Construction, for Canary Wharf Limited, so had thus reached the top of the world's biggest company in property development. After the business in the UK went into administration, to be launched again in 1993 under the chairmanship here of Lord Levene, he found himself as an executive director and then, in March 1997, as the only chief executive. Now he is also the chairman.

Getting his CBE in 2003 and becoming a trustee of the British Museum in 2007, it is hardly surprising that he sees himself as British as any Londoner. He shares a home here with his daughter. Lord Levene of Portsoken recommended Iacobescu to me as the man who knew Canary Wharf probably better than anyone else he knew. And Levene knows many people.

Both Levene and Iacobescu have private offices of the kind you would expect in films. By comparison, I have never seen Lord Heseltine in an office that anyone would envy. But all that glisters is not gold. Initial investors still wait for returns. Credit Suisse and Morgan Stanley were also early tenants. CWG shares fell 11 percent between their initial offering in 1999 to 2004, which is when Songbird took over control and re-launched on the alternative investment market with the support of Qatar and China; together with Morgan Stanley Real Estate and the New York investor Simon Glick, they own about 72 percent of the company at the time of writing about this.

This is 92 acres of property with 15.9m square feet of offices and a deal of retail space. Out of the 35 completed buildings they rent 17 to other companies, having sold the old Lehman Brothers building to JP Morgan Chase for £495m. Morgan plans to move all 8,000 of its workers there from the City of London in 2012. While the Lehman collapse cost CWG more than £50m in anticipated rent, it can boast it now hosts the most important banks, excluding Goldman Sachs, RBS, Deutsche Bank and UBS. Shell International is on its way. There is also a wealth of retail space, with Tiffany and Aquascutum as two of the latest tenants. It is virtually a town within a town, if not, as yet, officially a city.

Of course, Canary Wharf can offer better infrastructure to commercial tenants than in the shaky early days (poor transport then put most people off), but it still has to pay to attract. At the time of writing rental income averaged £37.50 per square foot, compared with £55 in the City of London. Both rates had improved, but the gap was still there and was growing ever wider. Passenger capacity could rise 50 percent when Crossrail is up and running, but not until 2017. Then Liverpool Street should be seven minutes away and Heathrow forty four. On the other hand, the Jubilee Line should see a 33 percent increase in peak time capacity, with more trains per hour, very much before that. CWG has paid large amounts to ensure that this will happen.

Perhaps the most remarkable development is the installation of the Crossrail station, if not under water, at least in the water of the northern West India Dock. A 256 metre long structure will lie on one side of this stretch of water with seven layers of space within it to contain the station, plus offices and shops, the equivalent of one of the neighbouring tower blocks, but lying on its side. Boats will still have room to pass. Ships must go elsewhere.

Iacobescu is understandably proud of continuing the

Olympia and York tradition of entirely self-contained tall building construction, controlling every part of the process from supply and build to legal services and not using costly sub-contractors. The idea, of course, is to guarantee delivery within a jointly specified time, as well as to pare down costs greatly, while using any available funds to add quality. This continues even after the build, so making it possible to add improvements, like ways of saving energy.

What has now become the Canary Wharf system has also become a saleable service, with contracts agreed to develop property outside the Canary Wharf estate, markedly in the City of London.

I asked George Iacobescu for an explanation of why, when property prices had been falling for some time across most of Britain, those in London continued to rise. He said, in effect, that there seemed to be a lot of funny money around, but little of it British. He showed no signs of regret.

The other Olympia and York initiative, of guaranteeing a steady stream of benefit to the local community beyond simply creating wealth, has also been continued by Canary Wharf, as evidenced by its annual reports on corporate responsibility.

When the president of France was told of the work that CWG had done in the community, he sent a minister to see what could be learned; the social problems with La Defense in Paris were causing much concern. She showed admiration for the various ways in which CWG was creating work, as well as business opportunities, for people who lived in the area. George Iacobescu's similar attempts to help his home land, Romania, with the encouragement of the ubiquitous Jacob Rothschild, plus Prince Charles, were not so good. It seems that Charles had put behind him his earlier views about tower blocks, in favour of helping some distant royal relatives. But little seems to have changed in that country since Iacobescu left. Communist-era habits prevail.

All the same, he remembers the Isle of Dogs when he visited it for the very first time, thinking, after living in Canada, how it felt very much like a ghetto. That feeling does not exist any more. He made it go away.

George Iacobescu

THE INHERITANCE
Just that

reating Canary Wharf cost money. It is hard to say exactly how much. But the marvellous truth about investment is that the interest seldom stops. When the LDDC officially ended in 1988 it left an inheritance in two forms. One was a strongly vital community, regenerated in many ways, with a ripple effect over much of the country. The other was a pot of unspent money and a number of tasks undone.

But the LDDC was not alone in helping needy friends and neighbours. The tradition brought by the Reichmann brothers of working with the local community wherever they put up massive buildings continues to this day. Of course, their company has changed its name, its ownership, and perhaps its direction, but Canary Wharf has the same objectives of giving as well as taking.

It is hard to tell which organisation contributed most to local well-being and it probably does not matter. But Canary Wharf is still alive, of course.

There two ways of defining inheritance. One is physical. The other is social. And there is no doubt that the Reichmann brothers took a clear lead in handling both. It was in charge of its own money, of course. On the other hand, the LDDC was launched with a very predominant physical brief, on the logical assumption that local governments were responsible for the rest. This overlooked the fact that local governments had far less finance. What they used to have had been taken away: development grants, business rates and so on. It took some time to work together, to share income more usefully.

Now that the LDDC has gone, a pot of roughly £8m dispenses its interest in the form of grants among more than a hundred different projects designed in some way to benefit the community. This has been run by Tracey Betts of the Isle of Dogs Community Foundation, from Jack Dash House, owned by Tower Hamlets and named after the dockers leader who (accidently) made this all so necessary: he put the final nail in the coffin of what was once a flourishing industry, making way, in the course of time, for the growth of financial services. Jack Dash still seems a hero, strangely.

Tracey Betts took on the job a year after the LDDC closed down and has done a lot to boost its coffers by attracting cash from local companies such as Morgan Stanley, State Street Bank, Barclays Capital and Credit Suisse. But this has not been helped by the growth of companies who like to see their name alone attached to local good works. On the other hand, some of them offer help quietly, such as seconding staff to work as school governors through the Education Business Partnership run from Toynbee Hall by Mike Tyler.

Foundation grants come from interest on the capital, which means that at times when interest rates are low, there is less finance on offer. Projects are preferred with long term objectives with the chance of improving growth.

Beyond the Isle of Docks, the borough of Newham has its own pot from the LDDC, now run by the Royal Docks Trust. In 1998 this was worth £2.7m for use basically on infrastructure, together with the gift of all land in the area then held by the LDDC. There was also a further £8m for what are described as community projects. Plus the Windsor Park Management Company, with funds set aside just for compensation against future claims of toxicity.

The Reichmanns, while Olympia and York survived, seemed to have donated £2.6m to a wide array of local causes, including skills training programmes. The groans had been loud from the many pressure groups apparently challenging all change that no local people were likely to benefit from a commercial activity for which they lacked specific skills. The Liberals then running Tower Hamlets persuaded the Reichmanns that the proper reaction was to set up a local training centre to develop just those skills. The Reichmanns, in the property business, agreed to pay for the technical training that would be most useful to them. This produced five hundred people equipped, it seems, to work in building.

The Canary Wharf Group has continued this theme. They have provided 8,000 square feet of offices since 2006 to be used by Skillsmatch, which at the time of writing has created 1,600 new jobs, working with Tower Hamlets and Lewisham Colleges, while paying £250,000 a year for higher education programmes. So far 450 local people have been offered jobs on site. They also make education grants, as well as run apprenticeship schemes. At a higher level, they have helped small local companies to new income worth £382m.

One way or another both organisations have made serious contributions to local welfare, such as funding for eleven new primary schools, two secondary schools and three colleges, as well as nine vocational training centres.

Corporate responsibility is a misused phrase, but it is hard to think of a better one. Especially when it happens.

SCHOOL REPORT
Evaluation

So was it all worth it? I use something I call the Embankment Test. If you wait for a train at Embankment station (the Underground, the District Line) and compare the faces of waiting passengers, those going east and those going west, it is generally true that those going west will point their eyes in an upward direction, while those going east look down. I read this as body language which shows that those who live in the west are more confident than those going east, if only because they are wealthier. And because they are wealthier they can have better houses and live in leafier areas. More belief in a better future.

Lately, however, what used to be constant has now become less certain. The faces of those who are travelling east, to Canary Wharf or anywhere near, have started to lift their eyes to the sky. This is the kind of sign that economists so often fail to spot.

So this is a measure of spiritual wealth. There are also financial measures, of course. Specific to Canary Wharf we have the claim from consultants to the Department of the Environment that the money spent on behalf of the public, £1.86bn over 17 years, was more than outpaced by private investment of £8.7bn, three quarters from overseas.

But the LDDC did not work alone. Other public funds

were invested. Such as £220m from London Transport, £669m from the Department of Transport for access roads outside of the LDDC area, and £1.3bn direct from the Treasury to ensure the success of the Jubilee Line. Then there is Crossrail, which is expected to cost £16b by its target completion in 2017, although of course Canary Wharf is not the sole beneficiary. But there is also the cost of the tax breaks to companies in the Enterprise Zone for ten years of roughly £3.9bn. This looks very much like a public investment of £24bn over the 17 years to 1998, against private investment of £8.7bn..

You can call it seed money if you like, but just how long do we need to wait to see the full plant grow? A government survey suggested the full benefit would not be seen until 2015, when the ratio of benefits should increase by a third. Tax income from companies outside the enterprise zone has no doubt logged up over the years, plus more when the zone's exemption expires, but still a gradual return, it seems.

A major claim to fame for Canary Wharf is that, as an urban development area, it got roughly ten times the amount of grant from central government than the ten others in the UK. It is fairly easy to see how this happened. It started as a modest attempt to improve an area for industrial development. But then, because of the sudden explosion of a new growth industry, financial services, it began to produce considerable wealth at a highly critical time. So when things went wrong, as they often do, it seemed foolish not to continue.

But did things go wrong through lack of direction or because the wrong people were put in charge? Was the relationship between the parties – national and local government, businesses and local people – sufficiently well designed? What lessons were learned for the future?

It is certainly true that property prices have seldom fallen in the east London area, no matter what happened in the country as a whole, which suggests a general confidence by investors in Canary Wharf.

Nevertheless, a recent survey of enterprise zones around the world suggests strict limits to what such schemes can produce. The Work Foundation in 2011 pointed out, first, the considerable cost of creating jobs, at an average of £23,000 each, presumably just in the UK. It also pointed out that, in many cases, they succeeded mainly in just moving jobs from one place to another. Only a quarter of the jobs were new. This report was published at just the time when a new British government had decided to extend the process more widely.

Having decided to end regional development agencies, the plan instead is to be more specific about those areas most in need and call them Local Enterprise Partnerships. One such is planned for the Royal Docks, at the east end of the old LDDC area, sometimes also called Thames Gateway. Business rates collected in those areas would be kept by partnerships for the next 25 years provided, of course, another government does not have another plan. Of course the main problem with the regional agencies was nothing much to do with geography, but mainly with the way they were run - as a cosy cabal of civil servants, with no system of allowing input from, for instance, school governors who are responsible for education, the key to much local improvement. Partnerships will do no better unless such problems are solved.

A recent survey by the University and College Union showed that a third of London constituencies have a very high proportion of unqualified adults. Hackney South and Shoreditch scored most poorly, with one in five lacking qualifications. Poplar and Limehouse and Bethnal Green and Bow scored better, with roughly one in ten. But this compares, for instance, with Brent North, where only 1.9 percent of adults do not have qualifications. It is hard to see how moving tax revenue in itself is going to help. All the same, East End educational standards have seen record improvements in recent years, no doubt boosted by an overall increase in finance from many sources.

Marks? Eight out of ten at the time of writing, despite the hidden cost of infrastructure.

There'll be another Embankment Test in a year.

THE PRODIGAL SON

An exception

The East End was never a total disaster. Poverty, of course, was common. So was, and is, overcrowding. Lack of education was a problem that only now is being corrected, with some of the best results in the country. But despite all that there are many examples of individual pluck and luck that give the lie to the misconception that East Enders lack the ability to develop new technical skills. Schools are clearly very important, but they are not the only educators.

Strangely enough, with Canary Wharf now seen as the world's financial centre, mainly with help from foreign investors, it is interesting that one of the world's richest men, who has made billions out of currency trading, was born in 1937 over a pub in the Roman Road, in the heart of the East End. He had left school at the age of fifteen with no obvious qualifications.

Joe Lewis is his name. Some in the business now call him The Boxer, partly because of his punchy nature, partly because his name almost matches the name of a famous fighter.

His father sold drink, but also food. They started a company called Tavistock Banqueting, first to cater for Masonic meetings, then to give tourists a taste of Olde England, albeit in the West End of London, with medieval banquets. Theme catering took off like a rocket. But it was obvious that many Americans who could not make the trip to London would like it just as much at home. So the business moved cross The Atlantic before the Canary Wharf project began.

The new business was called the Tavistock Group and rapidly diversified. Theme restaurants continued to boom, with Robert Earl, an assistant to Lewis, going on to found the Hard Rock Café and, later, Planet Hollywood. Lewis sold out of catering in 1979 and discovered a skill that he had not learned at school, trading money. How he did this is just not known, as he does not talk to journalists, but when the British pound crashed in 1992 it was not only the Hungarian George Soros who made a profit, but also the cockney Joe Lewis. Three years later it was repeated with the Mexican peso and he made another killing. This may be what dispassionate people in the business call taking a position.

At the time of writing he was said to have homes in four countries, including the Bahamas (for tax reasons, obviously), Argentina and Florida, while the company claimed investments in fifteen countries and 175 companies. These include: in Britain pubs again, sports with Tottenham Hotspur and gambling with Ladbrokes, and in the US yacht marinas, golf clubs and hospitals. Plus what was left of Icelandic banks.

Lewis' yacht, the *Aviva*, was moored by Tower Bridge while he made a bid for another pub chain. Visitors were impressed by the art on display by Picasso, Schiele and

Klimt. Not your normal nautical kit.

He has also lost money. For instance, 9.4 percent of the US bank Bear Stearns when it was in trouble, on the basis that failing banks are always bought out by somebody. That was true, but he had paid $107 a share, while JP Morgan took over the assets and paid only $10 a share, which is said to have cost Lewis over $1bn. But he could afford it. He hosts the Tavistock Cup golf tournament every March in Florida, owning three of the four clubs that compete, and once gave $1.4m to a charity to play golf with Tiger Woods. The two have reportedly stayed close ever since.

It is tempting to draw comparisons between Lewis and the Canary Wharf generator Michael von Clemm in their educational attitudes.

In the *Forbes* magazine US rich list Lewis came in at 347 and in the *Sunday Times* British list he came in at 22nd, valued at £2.8bn. Not bad for an East End drop out. Reminds me of my grandfather.

KEY WORDS

Isle of Dogs: The name given to the area that looks like a peninsular from the air and which was at one time almost an island apart from two connecting bridges. It originally housed most of the enclosed docks in the Port of London. Think of it as a Cinderella who will one day meet her prince.

East End: A title which many claim, but which is most often used to describe the area which is now contained within the London Borough of Tower Hamlets, including the Isle of Dogs. Tower Hamlets itself evolved from the boroughs of Poplar, Bethnal Green and Stepney, plus various parishes and boards of works.

Docklands: This described a wider area than the Isle of Dogs, to also include nearby open docks on both sides of the Thames, most recently controlled by the Port of London Authority before being handed over to the London Docklands Development Corporation.

Canary Wharf: Originally a wharf called Rum Quay, for unloading rum, that was renamed Canary Wharf to mark a better growth business of importing bananas and tomatoes from the Canary Islands. Now it is the name generally given to the area of development on what is geographically called the Isle of Dogs, but which I have extended to include all of the former development area north of The Thames

Canada Tower: What its owners call Number One Canada

Place, the first skyscraper to go up in Canary Wharf. On completion it was the tallest building in Britain. Canada comes into the equation through the original Canadian developers, Olympia and York. York comes from a place in Canada. Olympia from a brand of men's socks.

PLA: Port of London Authority, originally created to steer the interests of all London docks, but which has now shifted its focus to Tilbury, nearer the mouth of the Thames.

EDA: Economic development area, also called an enterprise zone. This is usually a fairly limited area designated by national government for the purposes of kick-starting commercial activity with a concentrated injection of preferential treatment, such as lifting taxation for, say, ten years, as well as the need for planning permissions. The idea was to encourage private enterprise. Not to be confused with UDCs.

Red roads: The roads initially built out of red bricks within the Docklands EDA, with the aim of speedily adding colour as well as convenience, as bricks were easily movable for later underground installations.

UDC: Urban Development Corporation, such as the London Docklands Development Corporation, an autonomous body created by the Conservative national government that for 17 years steered progress on the Isle of Dogs. This provided national finance to pay for expensive infrastructure, and then to sell off public land, to invest in the general area. UDCs were first used by a Labour government in Scotland and Wales in 1975.

LDA: London Development Agency. This is the body that inherited much of the unfinished business of the LDDC. This has overlapped over the years with English Partnerships and the Homes and Communities Agency. All of these have been threatened with closure as part of the attempted reduction in public spending and in unelected agencies.

GLC/GLA: The Greater London Council and the Greater London Authority, each of which at different times provided different levels of overall government structure for the greater London area.

DLR: The Docklands Light Railway, a driverless, computer-controlled transport system created by the Canadian company Bombardier. This started life and remains famous for making Skidoo snowmobiles. It is now one of the largest makers of rolling stock in the world.

Social housing: State owned housing originally provided at subsidised rates for the needy by the local authority, which was then called council housing. Much of this has now been removed from local authorities and handed over to semi-autonomous housing associations. The original aim was to remove finance for housing from government debt, so making the national economy look healthier.

Administration: if bankrupt, this means winding up and distributing anything left to creditors and, if not bankrupts, winding up and distribution to the owners. The type of supervision varies from country to country. In the US and Canada this is organised in different ways by the courts. In the UK the courts appoint an administrator, usually meaning a partnership of accountants.

EVENTS AS THEY HAPPENED

1939

3 September: Start of World War Two.

1940

7 September: On what was later to be called Black Saturday a German air raid blitzed the 43 miles of docks with 320 Heinkel and Dornier bombers, leaving 430 dead, 1,600 injured and 10,000 homeless. Much of the Isle of Dogs was destroyed. In London overall up to May 1941 some 3.5m homes were destroyed, killing 29,890 and injuring 50,497.

1944

6 June: 209 ships with 1,000 barges sail from the London docks down the Thames to deliver concrete Mulberry caissons for the invasion of France.

13 June: The first of many V1 rockets landed in the East End, eventually leading to even more deaths than in the blitz. A third of the population moved out of London, from the East End mainly to Essex. Ninety percent of those remaining moved into council built housing.

1945

May 8: End of second world war (VE Day) in Europe.

1951

Conservative national government elected.

1960

Highest ever cargo turnover for London docks, at 60m tons,

despite increasing use of containers elsewhere and industrial unrest led by unofficial, communist, trades union activists such as Jack Dash.

London Docks closed and infilled by the Port of London Authority.

1961

Crossbow magazine publishes article by Godfrey Hodgson describing the need for urban renewal agencies.

1964

Labour national government elected.

1965

The Greater London Council, Conservative led, succeeds the London County Council, while the London Borough of Tower Hamlets, led by Labour, is created out of the previous boroughs of Bethnal Green, Poplar and Stepney.

1967

Second Blackwall road tunnel opened.

1968

Greater London Council buys St Katherine's Dock from the PLA and starts development.

1969

March: *New Society* publishes an article, The Non-Plan, by Reyner Banham, Paul Barker, Peter Hall and Cedric Price suggesting that the best future for town planning depends on no planning, meaning that the will of individuals is usually better than an imposed central system.

Olympia and York Developments launched in Canada.

Surrey Docks sold by PLA to Southwark, which began a programme of infilling until the LDDC took over in 1981.

December: The GLC publishes a Greater London Development plan.

1970

Conservative national government elected.

Isle of Dogs independence movement launched by former docker and councillor Ted Johns, as president with two prime ministers, closing the two main access routes to the docks for ten days. His main motive was fighting national domination. Johns' father had reported for the *Daily Herald*, later to become *The Sun*, then a socialist newspaper part launched by George Lansbury, a radical mayor of Poplar.

1971

Dock workforce 6,000.

1973

GLC publish the Travers Morgan plan with five options suggested for the redevelopment of the docklands, a little east of London. Eight and a half square miles lay derelict, larger than the cities of London and Westminster combined.

St Katherine's Dock development opens.

A surge in the world price of oil depresses world stock markets and property prices and leads to world-wide inflation.

1974

Labour national government elected. Labour GLC elected.
Docklands Joint Committee set up by the GLC and five
London boroughs.

1976

DJC produces a 20-year strategic plan for a Docklands
Development Corporation with the stress on public housing
and transport, while the South East Economic Planning
Council unsuccessfully advises the Labour government to set
up a development corporation.

1978

The idea of enterprise zones is launched in a speech to the
Bow Group by Conservative MP Geoffrey Howe.

1979

Conservative national government elected. Parliamentary
committee blames DJC for doing nothing. London
Docklands Development Corporation is proposed by
Conservative minister Michael Heseltine.

Olympia and York buy English Properties in the UK.

1981

LDDC is launched as an unelected administrative agency
with overriding powers to inspire economic regeneration of
5,503 acres of the docklands (although the word
regeneration is not used), with an annual grant of £90m. It is
the biggest of its kind in Europe. Sir Nigel Broakes,
chairman of property company Trafalgar House also

becomes chairman of LDDC and Bob Mellish, a Labour MP is made his deputy. Chief executive is Reg Ward, a former council CEO. A strategy is drawn up by Coopers and Lybrand which anticipates a lifespan of between 10 and 15 years. The actual lifespan was 17 years.

With the increasing use of containers worldwide for cargo, the workforce in the outdated London docks drops to 3,000.

Limehouse Television Studios move into Shed 30 on Canary Wharf and stay until 1989.

Proposal delivered for London City Airport.

LDDC announce plans for 480 homes in Beckton.

Council houses available to new tenants in London are cut by 41 percent between 1981 and 1989, while council house building is cut by 91 percent and 17 percent of existing council houses are sold. Private landlord annual income from council tenants rises from £4m to £99m. There are 6,000 registered as homeless in Tower Hamlets, while those sleeping rough nightly are said to number 250.

Social Democratic Party formed in Limehouse.

1982

Enterprise zone covering about one tenth or 482 acres of the northern end of the docklands, created by Conservative chancellor Geoffrey Howe, launched with a 10 year lifespan, offering generous tax, rates and planning concessions.

Two new light railway routes agreed, running from Tower Hill and Stratford, largely reclaiming ancient bridges and tracks previously used for ship to shore coal transport. The government grant is £77m. Many bridges need reinforcement.

LDDC produces a development design guide, which is quickly forgotten. Chief planner Gordon Cullen resigns.

Billingsgate fish market makes its pre-arranged move from the City of London to a 13 acre site on the Isle of Dogs.

Thames Barrier opened.

Docks workforce numbers 600.

After local elections produce stronger left wing Labour councils, Newham, Tower Hamlets and Southwark withdraw their official representatives from the LDDC.

1983

A new, red brick public road costing £2.5m is built on Marsh Wall, part of the enterprise zone. Northern and Shell, the British franchise owners of *Penthouse* magazine and I move in fast.

An ASDA super store opens.

Conservatives win another general election.

Royal assent given for the DLR, expected to cost £77m.

1984

A dedicated bus service starts running to CW from Mile End station.

Nigel Broakes resigns as chairman of LDDC in favour of Sir Christopher Benson, until 1988.

Over a good lunch on the floating restaurant Res Nova, moored next to Shed 31, the idea is born of persuading financial companies to move to Canada Wharf. Those present included Reg Ward, LDDC chief executive, Michael von Clemm, chairman of Credit Suisse First Boston and Archibald Cox, chairman of Morgan Stanley.

1985

Short takeoff and landing airport, privately owned, approved by government to fly from Royal Docks.

Work starts on the Canary Wharf Master Building Project. Work starts on Docklands Light Railway, to be run by London Transport.

John Mills leaves Camden Council to become LDDC deputy chairman with the brief to improve local links.

The proportion of British people living in poverty rises to 17 percent, an increase by 55 percent over 1979. In the East End poverty effects one third of the population.

1986

Liberal/SDP party takes control of Tower Hamlets (until 1994) and promptly devolves the area into seven sections, each with its own town hall and some under Labour leadership. TH joins board of LDDC.

Financial services in the UK deregulated, the 'Big Bang'. GLC dissolved.

News International moves to Wapping.

A new access road, the Limehouse Link, is approved, agreed with an estimated cost of £41m but by 1992 costing over £100m, plus £30m given to Tower Hamlets for social improvements, making it the most expensive road ever built. 550 families had to be moved through compulsory purchase.

The LDDC's planning committee for the first time admits the public to its meetings.

The City of London reacts to Canary Wharf by granting planning permission for 17m square feet of new office space.

1987

July: Canary Wharf building, of 12.2m square feet on 20 acres, agreed between Paul Reichmann of the Canadian developers Olympia and York (who took over from Credit Suisse First Boston) and the LDDC, as part of a total 71 acre development. The overall price paid is £1m an acre, with £8m in cash and the rest in facilities. The architect is to be the Argentinean American Cesar Pelli.

The Queen opens the computer controlled DLR in 30 July, but technical problems prevent it from starting until 31 August. Estimated passenger use grows from 1,500 a day to 13,000, so new contracts have to be issued. Trains grow from one to two cars.

The Queen opens London City Airport.

Reg Ward is helped by government minister Michael Portillo to step down as CEO of LDDC in favour, eventually, of Michael Honey. In between control is held by Major General Rougier, who surrenders after 16 days. Four other senior managers resign.

The LDDC reaches agreement with the Borough of Newham on working together. Newham joins LDDC board.

Black Monday on October 29 sees the London stock market crash by 26 percent, severely affecting property prices.

First flight leaves London City Airport for Paris.

1988

May: Canary Wharf build begun by Paul Reichmann's Olympia and York Canary Wharf Limited as the world's largest new property development.

July: Chancellor Nigel Lawson ends double mortgage tax relief, leading to a collapse in property prices for four years, imprisoning many with negative equity. New mortgages are charged at 15 percent.

Select committee of MPs urges change of direction for the LDDC. The corporation broadens its role and recruits more staff to launch what is to become a community services division, dealing with education, health, welfare, tourism, arts, leisure and social housing, with the planned support of five percent of the corporation's annual budget.

1989

DLR extension work to Beckton begins.

Jubilee line extension to Canary Wharf and Stratford approved.

Homelessness in Tower Hamlets is registered at ten times the national average.

LDDC reaches agreement with the London borough of Tower Hamlets on working together and itself becomes a housing development association.

1990

Topping out ceremony at CW is disturbed by sheep and bees released by local residents in protest against lack of local consultation.

Agreement reached to extend DLR to Greenwich.

Thames Barrier begins construction.

London councils become educational authorities.

LDDC agrees a code of consultation with local councils. Councillors join the planning committee.

More teenagers, 500, are notified as runaways at Limehouse police station than in the whole remainder of the region; 56 of them are under twelve.

1991

August: First CW commercial tenants move in.

Michael Heseltine announces extension of LDDC principle to the Thames Gateway.

Department of Environment rejects latest LDDC corporate plan and parachutes in Eric Sorensen from central government and the Liverpool UDC to become CEO.

DLR carries 32,000 passengers a day and is taken over by LDDC with Lord Levene as chairman. A 1.6km extension is opened to reach Bank station. 11 cars are sold and 70 new cars are delivered.

Approval given to extend runway for the use of jets at London City Airport.

London commercial property market collapses.

1992

May: Only half of Canada Tower is let. O&Y goes into administration in Canada with $20bn of debt. The corporate collapse in the UK sets a national record.

London City airport extension opens with 192 flights a year.

1993

May: Limehouse road link opens.

Conservative government re-elected. Lord Levene becomes chairman of both DLR and LDDC until 1996.

September: A semi-literate BNP candidate gets elected to Tower Hamlets Council for eight months.

October: O&Y, trading as Canary Wharf Group, recovered from administration by banks, who put in another £1.1bn. This is also jointly chaired by Lord Levene, for the bank-owned holding company called Sylvester Investments.

December: Jubilee line extension begins, at a cost of £1,000m, with a contribution from CW.

Workers number about 7,000, with 15 shops.

1994

Workers number about 12,800, with 27 shops.

Labour regains control of Tower Hamlets. The BNP councillor leaves the area.

1995

June: DLR starts working at weekends, carries 50,000 daily passengers

December: CWG sold back to Paul Reichmann and others

for £800m.

LDDC withdraws from Southwark.

London City Airport handles 0.5m annual passengers.

CW workers number 13,000, with 42 shops.

1996

IRA bomb explodes at South Quay.

DLR extension to Lewisham opens.

LDDC gives Beckton back to Newham.

1997

Labour national government elected. Workers number about 25,000.

Docklands Railway Management takes over DLR from LDDC for four years.

Wapping, Limehouse and the Isle of Dogs given back to Tower Hamlets.

Local residents fail in appeal to House of Lords, claiming that Canada Tower interferes with television reception.

LDDC hands back Wapping and Limehouse to the borough of Tower Hamlets.

1998

LDDC hands back the Royal Docks and some cash to Newham and is itself dissolved. Remaining assets are passed to English Partnerships, a part of the Department of the Environment.

Government approves DLR extension to London City Airport.

City Airport is allowed up to 73,000 flights a year, with 1.3m passengers.

CWG, formerly Sylvester Investments, relisted on the London Stock Exchange, valued at £1.4 billion.

Financial Services Authority moves to Canary Wharf.

1999

Jubilee line extends to Green Park and Stanmore, half paid for by CWG.

Serco buys DLR.

CW workers number about 27,000, with 90 shops.

February: CW 99% let. Canada Place shopping mall opens, including Boots, Tesco and Waitrose.

CWG valued by Forbes Magazine at $4bn.

September: Jubilee line station at CW opens.

November: DLR extends to Lewisham at a cost of £200m

December: Workers number about 55,000.

2000

An elected Greater London Authority created, led by Conservatives.

Excel exhibition centre opens. Millennium Dome opens.

2001

Transport for London take control of DLR.

2002

DLR buys 24 new rail cars ahead of the London City Extension.

2003

December : 60,000 workers, 200 shops.

2004

CW group, now Britain's biggest property company, is sold to Songbird Estates, whose biggest shareholder is the sovereign wealth fund for Qatar. CW relisted on the London Stock Exchange's Alternative Investment Market.

DLR is extended to London City Airport.

December: 82,000 workers.

2006

December: 90,000 workers, of whom 25 percent live in the nearest five boroughs.

2007

DLR carries 60 million passengers a year.

June: Crossrail link finally agreed by government, to connect the eastern to the western outer parts of London by 2018 at a cost of £15.9bn, including a stop at Canary Wharf, towards which CWG will contribute £150m. There will be 24 trains an hour in each direction. Crossrail will be Europe's biggest building structure.

City airport reports 3m annual passengers.

Millennium Dome re-opened as the O2 Centre.

December: 93,000 workers at CW.

2008

DLR starts using three car trains, plus a programme of further platform enlargement ahead of the bid for the

Olympics in Stratford 2012. A programme of regular weekend closures begin, both for DLR and London Underground, ahead of track improvements needed for the London Olympics. City Airport handles 3.3m passengers a year.

2009

Conservative and Liberal Democrat national government elected.

CASH FLOW

The National Audit Office produced this comparative chart to show how monies moved in and out of the London Docklands Development Corporation between 1981 and 1998, which was its lifetime. Different lines indicate different cash flows.

The big numbers on the graph show peak moments:

1 shows the cost of building the Limehouse Link, the most expensive road in Europe;

2 shows the start of winding up, including disbursements to local authorities;

3 shows the time when the central grant was reduced as a result of rising income from selling land;

4 shows a rise in administrative costs caused by changing the nature of LDDC business;

5 shows a rise in activity caused by the start of the DLR;

6 shows a fall in income after a national decline in the value of property;

7 shows rising income from the DLR.

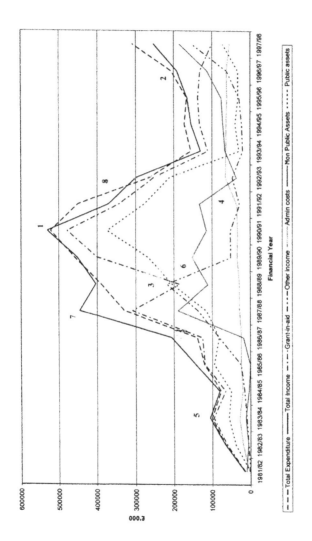

PROGRESS

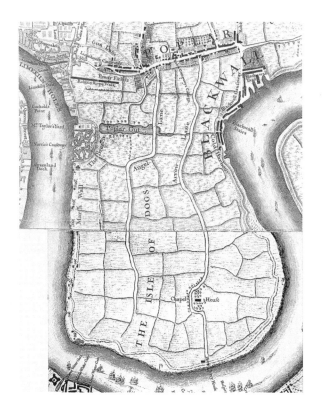

1745

A close look will show: boats with sails, windmills on Marsh Wall to pump out marsh water, the Blackwall to block out river water, Limekilns where the famous porcelain was made, and the India Company's College for training sailors. There were few roads and not many houses.

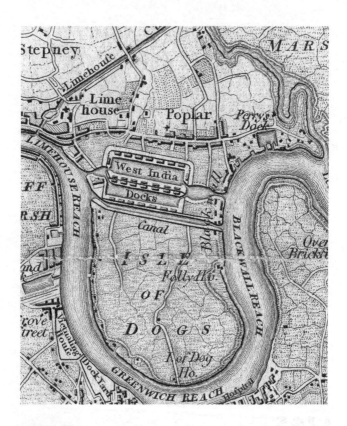

1801

Millwall docks had not happened, but there were two West India docks. East India docks were then called Perry's dock. Poplar cut had become a canal. There was one house at the southern tip.

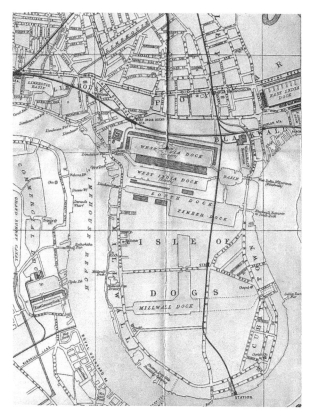

1875

East India dock had arrived. There was now West India dock import and West India dock export. Poplar cut had become South dock and Timber dock. Millwall dock had also been created. So had steam driven railways.

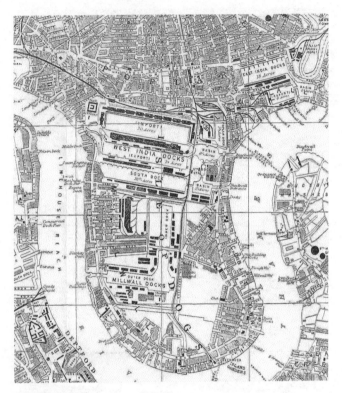

1952

This was after the Second World War, with the docks doing record business. East India docks import covered 18 acres and export 8. West India docks import covered 30 acres, export 24 and south docks 20. There were also the basins for manoeuvring traffic. Compare these with the next map.

NOW

North and South docks remain, if slimmer, less the Crossrail station sunk into the North dock. West India export dock is much truncated, being largely replaced by Jubilee park and various other encroachments. Aspen Way is the major trunk road improving vehicle access to the area, directly leading to the Limehouse Link. The DLR is fully active, even reaching across The Thames.

INSPIRATION

This report is not the first to be written about Canary Wharf in the context of London, although it is meant to the first of a kind in balancing principle forces. So it is right to give credit to sources.

Essential is the detailed website recording the work of the LDDC, so carefully compiled by Stuart Innes: *www.lddc-history.org.uk*.

An efficient academic treatise, while not perfect, is *Connection to the world*, by Lane and Foster at Cornell University. This was first to recognise the area as a city: *www.barrett-lane.com*.

By far the most coherent consideration of Canary Wharf as a planning process, in terms of both design and organisation, is spelt out in *London Docklands* by Brian Edwards, a lecturer in urban design at Strathclyde University. One instance of confusion between Hackney and Tower Hamlets can easily be forgiven.

Developing London's Docklands by Sue Brownill openly describes both its aim and its conclusion with the sub-title *Another great planning disaster*? Prejudice aside, it has a deal of data which is important to the total picture.

Some Lives, by David Widgery, is typical of numerous books, based on a singular view of the area. Widgery was a local doctor, as well as a very active journalist with very strong left wing views. He wrote from the heart about local poverty but, as was observed in his *Guardian* obituary, he was not a man to allow mere facts to get in the way of a story.

Very much more factual was the detailed survey by Janet Foster called *Docklands*, the result of a couple of years of work essentially drawing on hundreds of interviews. This was supported by a deal of data and many references to other specialists on civic regeneration.

The architecture was well-described by Stephanie Williams in her work *The docklands*, even though produced midway through development. Much less successful was *A vision of Britain* by HRH the Prince of Wales, who admits his knowledge of the subject is slight. He also does not seem to know that Bow is in the East End, which makes his views on this bit of development, though thoughtful, not very helpful.

Gathering data on Olympia and York, the vehicle for the Reichmann brothers, who finally realised Canary Wharf, was considerably helped by the brilliant *Too big to fail*, published in Canada by Walter Stewart. Not entirely accurate, it all the same details key causes and effects.

Most valuable, perhaps, in helping to shape the set of values hopefully applied in this book was a work by the critic V S Pritchett, published fifty years ago in the USA, called *London Perceived*. This erudite and graceful work, thoroughly covering all of London, impressed this author with the need to call on every aspect of what is called culture to evaluate any physical entity. His has been possibly the best book ever in capturing the spirit of London at large. At least, that is my personal opinion. This report is just a shadow.

THE AUTHOR

Kevin d'Arcy is an award-winning broadcaster who was previously editor and publisher of *Spokesman*, the international review of policy and media. He has worked for the BBC in Britain and CBC in Canada. He was the first managing editor of the monthly *Nova*. He has also worked for *The Economist* and the *Financial Times* and was head of public relations for the National Economic Development Office. His previous books include *The Voice of the Brain of Britain*, a profile of Radio Four, and *Who's in charge here?*, about democracy in Britain today, also published by Rajah Books.

AND FRIENDS

None of this would have been possible without the strong support and honest criticisms of fellow enthusiasts Celia Hampton, Tim Cheatle and Paul Hodgson. The author is also grateful to Michael Evans, Paul Martin and David Barker, as well as to Kevan Collins, Mike Tyler, Jonathan Fryer and Charlotte Iseline.